HITTING THE ROAD

CW00847515

Motorcycle travels o

Author: Jacek Klimko

First published: March 2017.

Copyright (C) 2017 by Jacek Klimko

Cover design Copyright (C) 2017 by Jacek Klimko

Table of contents:

A bag of luck

Death behind the corner

Leaving home

Farewell

About us... where it all started

Bear with us

"If people never did silly things nothing intelligent would ever get done."

by Ludwig Wittgenstein

Our honeymoon was slowly coming to an end. There were only a few more days left to roam.

We spent most of our two-week holiday in Romania and around the Carpathian mountains. Later we drove our motorcycle through Hungary, which was a stark contrast to where we'd come from. It was more expensive, less interesting and flat as a pancake. Luckily entering Slovakia was a welcomed change of scenery. Slovak hills and bendy roads proved to be a real pleasure to navigate. When tired, the unspoiled nature offered us fine spaces for rest and camping. In our element, we wanted this adventure to last forever. We were eager to take full advantage of our honeymoon adventure, right up to the very last day.

It was the beginning of September and soon to be Rebecca's birthday. For that special day we planned to find a romantic spot for wild camping. We hoped to come across something isolated and picturesque at the same time. It was meant to be a perfect evening, with tasty snacks, nature and each other's company. It was the kind of simple living that appealed to us. There was nothing else we needed, nor wanted.

Around late afternoon we'd just started looking for a campsite when out of nowhere, by the side of the road, we came across a young couple. There was something odd about the situation. The moment they saw us, their hands went up in a frantic attempt to stop us. I hit the brakes and they ran towards the motorcycle. They looked distressed. "Could you help us?" were the first words we heard. They were tourists from India who'd got lost and didn't know what to do. Unfortunately, hitching a ride was proving to be a challenge for them as nobody wanted to stop in the middle of nowhere. As we were chatting, a loud scream came from within a short distance of us. We all spun round and saw two girls on bicycles heading in our direction. Right in front of them was a large black bear with two cubs running across the road. Thankfully, the bears disappeared into the forest within seconds, but it was enough to leave all of us stunned. This brief encounter scared everyone, but for the Indian couple it was just all too much for one day. They probably wanted nothing more than to be back in a city, where they'd feel safe. We decided to help them. I managed to stop a passing car and after explaining the situation to the driver, to the couple's relief, I bagged them a ride to the nearest city. Soon we were standing there on our own, thrilled that we'd seen bears so close up. Rebecca pulled out her camera hopeful that the animals would still be around, hiding somewhere, but they were long gone. For me it was a great relief. I was scared that the mother could easily turn aggressive trying to protect her cubs. We drove off knowing that we were in bear territory.

About an hour later we found just the right spot for our campsite. There were mountains everywhere, most of the land was covered by lush forest and there were no houses around. It felt like we were in the middle of a national park. We got off the main road and drove up a small, unpaved path. We soon came upon a large open space located on a hillside. We drove across the field to the far end and stopped at the edge of the forest, completely out of sight. It was a million star hotel in the middle of nowhere, and it was all ours. It was an excellent find. There was still plenty of time before dusk. Slowly, we pitched our tent and I covered the motorcycle for the night. Rebecca joined our sleeping bags together and made the bed. Soon we were eating our supper while sitting on the grass enjoying the sunset.

All was great, except that the bears were still on my mind. I was worried about a potential uninvited visit in the middle of the night. I couldn't hide it and Rebecca sensed my anxiety. I wanted to be protective over my new wife, but it quickly turned into an obsession. First, I began to move our stuff from the tent back onto the motorcycle. It was easy to agree that any food should not stay in the tent, but soon I started moving other things, like toothpaste, toothbrushes (these contained traces of toothpaste) and anything that was even remotely related to food, like for example a knife, which I had used to cut bread. I had no idea how sensitive a bear's sense of smell could be, but I didn't want to take even the tiniest risk. I think it was too much for Rebecca when I suggested that we should sleep with our motorcycle helmets next to us. She thought that the idea was crazy, while I saw it as a way to survive a bear attack. It was the final straw, the romance was dead. We turned our torches off, ready to sleep, but my thoughts still raced, keeping me wide awake.

We'd wild camped many times before, but that night my imagination was running away with me. During other camping adventures, I'd learned not to worry about humans. They seem to be relatively rational, most of the time, but dealing with wild animals was different. For me they were unpredictable, and that scared the shit out of me.

Pitching our tent on the edge of the forest had at first seemed ideal for a romantic night, but it turned out to be a bad choice. Soon after the sun had set, the trees came alive with all sorts of strange noises. Every little sound made me jump and I was imagining the worst. In my mind I saw the newspaper headline "missing travellers found weeks later after being mauled by hungry bears, bodies yet to be identified". In the end exhaustion took over and gradually pacified my mind. Unwillingly, I fell asleep. We hadn't been sleeping for long, most likely less than an hour, before we were suddenly awoken by a loud growling. That was it, undeniably a bear and not a happy one either. Shit, we were in serious trouble. I could no longer reason with my mind; it certainly wasn't just my imagination creating growling sounds near the tent.

Pushing my luck

Laying flat inside the tent, I was waiting for the inevitable to happen; for bears to come inside and eat us alive. I had a small pocket knife with me and I opened it up, ready to defend our lives. I did wonder, however, if I'd have a chance to fight off a bear with just a pocket knife, or would it be better to play dead... I was glad I'd insisted on having our helmets with us. With them by our sides, the strategy of acting dead seemed more plausible. Another option was to use my little knife to cut a hole in the tent and then run as fast as our legs would carry us. For hours I was considering every possible scenario. It sounds crazy now, but back then I was very serious; after all I was convinced there were bears nearby, just waiting for the chance to gobble up two juicy humans.

The growling echoed around the forest for hours, into the early morning. It stopped once the first sun had come up and we could finally come out of our tent. There were no bears in sight. We both breathed a sigh of relief; we had survived the night and were safe. But after a sleepless night, instead of packing up and leaving right away, we decided to get back in the tent to get some rest. We stayed inside until the sun made it unbearably hot. Then we had no choice. We had to move on. As always, we divided our duties and started packing up. Rebecca stayed around the tent and I went to the motorcycle. When I uncovered it, I noticed that the food bags were untouched. There was no evidence of curious, roaming bears. The bike had stayed shaded and was still wet from the morning dew. I sat on it, pulled the choke, turned the key and pressed the ignition button. Despite its age, the motorcycle was pretty reliable and always started first time. Not this day, though. I pressed the ignition again, and again, and again… and I kept trying until the battery was almost flat.

Before continuing, I remembered what had happened two weeks earlier in Ukraine. The situation was similar; after a night of camping I tried to start the bike but forgot that I'd turned the fuel tap off. By the time I realised my mistake, it was too late, the battery was dead. I pulled some seriously old Lada over and asked the driver for help. He didn't have cables with him, but managed to tear some wires from a nearby fence. That was the best he could find. He wrapped a cloth around the wires to avoid being electrocuted and jump started the bike. With that story in mind, I once again checked that the fuel tap was open. It was. The choke was in the right position, too. So I tried again. Nothing! I managed to try two more times before the battery died. That was it! We were stuck in the middle of nowhere.

The only solution I could think of was to move the bike back onto the road and push start it. This idea quickly turned out to be easier said than done. The nearest hardened path was about two hundred yards uphill. The field was soft, wet and grassy which made the whole endeavour helplessly discouraging. The sun was scorching hot, which didn't help either. It was going to be a long and difficult day. I quickly learned that pushing the bike straight up the hill was impossible. It refused to move in that direction. Luckily, the field was wide enough for me to zigzag the bike to the side and back, allowing me to make slow and painful progress up the hill. The method was working, but we were beginning to run out of energy, patience and water.

Rebecca tried helping as much as she could, but the sun was too strong for her and after some time she had to hide in the shade. The joys of being married to a redhead! I struggled on my own. It took over two hours of hard labour to get the bike to the top of the field, but I'd finally made it onto solid ground. It was a slow and painful victory, but there was no time for celebration. There was another task at hand; push starting the engine. The path was unpaved but hard enough to gain momentum. The problem was that I'd never started a bike this way before. I understood the principles but wasn't sure about the details. It didn't take long to realise that these small details were key to success. The only way to learn was by trial and error.

Reaching the right speed was the easiest part, while starting the bike proved to be the hardest. To begin with I put the bike in first gear, but each time I released the clutch, the back tyre locked. I tried second gear, but it made no difference. Something wasn't working and I didn't know what. I lost count of how many times I went up and down that path; twenty, thirty, maybe more. I was physically and mentally exhausted. At one point something broke in me. I threw the bike to the ground and disappeared into the forest. It was too much; my frustration had reached its limits. I sat on my own, leaning against a tree. I needed to remove myself from the situation, even if only for a moment. Angry and defeated, I was swearing and feeling sorry for myself. I needed to be left alone and didn't want to talk to Rebecca. She knew she was better off staying away. If she'd come over, we'd have only ended up arguing. I sat there for over half an hour and it somehow helped. I pulled myself together and went back to the bike. There was no other choice, I had to start again. It was long past noon and neither of us fancied spending another night surrounded by bears. With newfound willpower, I picked the bike off the ground and pushed it up the path. Again, I was doing everything I could to get us out of there. The engine was responding, but it wasn't starting. I knew that I could do it, so I continued pushing the bike up that bloody path.

I was failing time after time but refused to give up, until at one point, by what seemed a miracle, the engine started. In fact it wasn't a miracle. I'd cracked it. This time the bike was in the right gear, also the speed was right, I let go and quickly reapplied the clutch in just the right way, at the right moment, simultaneously twisting the throttle and hitting the ignition button. The day was almost over, sweat was dripping off my body, we were hungry and thirsty, but in the end I had done something that had seemed hopeless. I felt like Edison, failing my way to success, except that in the end I discovered something that I should have already known.

Needless to say, Rebecca's birthday wasn't exactly what we'd had in mind. It was meant to be a quiet romantic evening, but it turned into a series of unfortunate circumstances. One thing is sure, we'll remember that night for the rest of our lives.

A few days after our unforgettable night with bears, we were staying in a hotel in northern Slovakia. In winter it operated as a ski resort, positioned right in the middle of a mountain range. As we were checking in, we looked at the lobby TV. The news channel was on. They were reporting an unusually high level of bear activity in the region. The footage showed bears coming out of their natural habitat and rummaging through bins. Watching this news report only confirmed that our bear encounter a few evenings previously had been genuine, and that we'd been lucky to survive to tell the story.

That night we slept in a comfortable bed. It was a warm night and the air was filled with the smells of the nearby forest. We left the big windows wide open. Not long after falling asleep, we were woken up by a familiar growling coming from outside. We sprung out of bed, curious to see the offending animal. Being in the safety of the hotel, we ran to the windows looking for the bears. The night was brightened by a full moon, but we still couldn't see much. We ran to the lobby for a better view.

It was almost two o'clock at night and everyone was in bed, except the receptionist. The view from the lobby was better, but even though we knew the noise was coming from behind some bushes we still couldn't see anything. We gave up and started chatting to the receptionist. Before we'd have a chance to tell him about our "brave" encounter in the tent, he told us that the growling noise was from stags. I instantly realised that all that anxiety I'd experienced a few nights before had been for nothing. We were never in danger. It was all just a figment of the imagination. We went back to bed with mixed emotions: happy that we'd found out what the animal was, relieved that it hadn't been a bear, but also a bit disappointed for the very same reason.

Time for a change

Since returning from our honeymoon, the idea of pursuing a motorcycle-travel lifestyle had been slowly growing inside us. Our first experience was short, but it awakened our hunger for more adventure. The simplicity of life on the road was what we really enjoyed. It was a world of freedom and adventure. Not much back home could match that. After returning to work, we both knew that it was just a matter of time before we'd set off again. We hoped that the next time it would be for good.

A couple of years on we'd had enough of living comfortably and I was done with working as an IT project manager. I knew I wasn't interested in climbing up the corporate ladder. I was stressed out and dissatisfied. We had all we needed in terms of material things, but it wasn't what we wanted. There was only one solution, to alter our lifestyle. We decided to sell pretty much everything we owned, pack up and leave. For us it was a perfectly rational decision, but some branded us crazy. We felt sane and didn't feel the need to justify our choice; some understood us, most didn't and that was that. We didn't care what people thought or said. What we felt was more important, and we needed the change. We were eager to find something greater, more meaningful and adventurous than our life as it was.

Unprepared as we were, we decided to embark on a motorcycle odyssey. For a start, our experience of travelling on a motorcycle was limited. The motorcycle itself was nearly a quarter of a century old. My mechanical skills were pretty much non-existent; I just about knew how to check the oil level (any repair work was beyond me). As for the gear, we couldn't afford quality equipment and had to make do with the cheap stuff we already had, most of which was not suitable for a long journey. But none of that was going to stop us; we were decided.

Moving forward, we put almost everything we owned for sale. It was a way to finance our adventure. Also, we wanted to reduce the amount of possessions we had. But letting go of things we'd been collecting for years wasn't easy. In a way they were part of our identity. We soon realised that our choice to live a homeless life and travel on our motorcycle around the world was pretty radical, and it meant that we couldn't have it both ways; it was one way or the other. We couldn't cling to stuff we didn't really need. Besides we had no intention of settling down again so there was no point in keeping things "just in case", not even things of sentimental value. In the end we sold anything for which we could get some money. What we couldn't sell, we gave away for free. Some other things we donated to charity. We left a couple of suitcases of clothes in my parents' house, but that was it. We got rid of everything else. We downsized from a modern one-bed apartment to a two-man tent, improvised kitchen and a hole in the ground for a toilet. With everything gone, that was it, we were homeless with our rusty trusty motorcycle. Despite that, the whole experience felt liberating and refreshing.

New home

Our motorcycle and tent became our new home. The tent wasn't anything special. We'd bought it in a discount shop for less than twenty pounds. We couldn't complain, though. Even though it was a bit heavy, it was easy to pitch, almost entirely waterproof, had plenty of space inside and even a little porch to keep our kitchen bags and boots and stuff.

Our motorcycle was over twenty years old, but regardless of its age, was still pretty reliable. Before leaving Poland, we thought about getting a newer better bike, but in the end decided against the idea. We didn't want to spend extra money; money we didn't really have, and anyway, driving an old motorcycle worth just over a thousand pounds had its advantages. One of which was the low-tech carburettor engine. Being very simple and without any unnecessary electronics, it was relatively easy to fix by anyone with some basic mechanical skills, even by the side of the road. Another reason was that we weren't financially attached to it. It was just a tool, a means to our adventure, not an end. Even before setting off on this trip, we'd covered almost twenty thousand miles on it, so in our eyes the bike had already paid for itself. If it died on the way, we could simply scrap it and move on. Also in almost every country we visited, locals wanted to know how much the motorcycle was worth. Personally, I think I would have felt embarrassed to admit its worth if the bike had a really high value. Trying to explain that in Poland the age of the bike decided its value, always made for a good conversation. I would often be told that the amount I'd paid was less than the price of a scooter. The only problem was the

BMW sign. It screamed "expensive" and some people refused to believe that I'd paid so little for it, even to the point of arguing that I'd clearly got my numbers mixed up.

The bike was old and cheap, but that's not to say that I didn't care for it. I made sure that everything was in working order. This machine was to be our home for many years to come, so preparing it for the journey turned into one of the most important and challenging tasks. Any changes had to be functional, lightweight, durable and relatively inexpensive at the same time. I spent many long hours in the garage and probably even more in front of the computer doing research.

For example, choosing new side panniers took me over two months. I knew that whatever the choice, we would have to live with them for years. It was going to be our main luggage space, so it was important to get it right. There were a few things to consider. We wanted our panniers to be secure and durable, but at the same time lightweight and waterproof. Price also mattered. And the size had to be just right; not too little, not too large. It didn't take me long to realise that I'd have to compromise somehow.

To complicate the matter further, online biker communities were polarised on the subject of motorcycle panniers, and reading their comments made me even more confused. It seemed, though, that the mainstream trend was to use aluminium panniers. I remember reading "Long way round" many years earlier and wanting to be and look just like those guys from the cover photograph. The image of their large BMW motorcycles equipped with aluminium boxes stuck with me for years. Still to this day, aluminium panniers are an unquestioned standard, almost synonymous with motorcycle adventure. Not surprisingly, the aluminium was my first choice. We probably would have ended up with them, if not for the cost. Because they are so popular, they are expensive. The better they are, the more they cost. Anyway, from what I read these boxes are far from ideal in spite of the price; they bend, break and leak, and are pretty heavy at the same time.

On the other side of the argument were those who worship soft saddle bags. This subculture seemed an alternative to the mainstream trend, a voice of rebellion against mindlessly following fashion. If nothing else, it provided a choice. Soft being light, this option has its place, but it wasn't for us as it offered little security against theft or damage. We wanted to carry a small laptop and a camera with us, so needed something sturdier.

One day I came across Pelican panniers. They were plastic but looked strong enough for what we needed. It wasn't a motorcycle product but was easily adaptable. These boxes were durable, relatively cheap, much lighter than standard aluminium panniers and secure. That was it; I made a choice and ordered two 35L boxes from the US, where they're produced. I'd lose that Ewan McGregor adventurer look, but I had to be pragmatic about it and choose what was right for us.

When the boxes arrived a few weeks later, I saw how little space we'd have. Packing everything we had into those two boxes turned out to be completely unrealistic. I panicked. More space was urgently needed. Luckily we still had the old saddle bags from our honeymoon trip, so it was easy to experiment. That was it, I'd found a solution. With two Pelicans at the back and two soft bags at the front of the bike, we had more than enough space. Our home was complete.

We ended up with one hard box per person. It wasn't much space, not more than a small rucksack. It was just about enough room for a few personal items and any expensive or fragile things, like electronics and our camping stove. Other things that could be easily replaced and were relatively cheap were to be kept at the front, together with kitchen equipment and food. Our tent, sleeping bags, mat and a tarp were neatly packed in a large duffle bag, which I securely attached just behind Rebecca. There was also a small tool box, I'd made from a cheap PVC pipe, which I tucked away behind one of the boxes.

Now the biggest problem was the weight. The motorcycle was overloaded. Every single item on our packing list was carefully chosen and had to be justified. We packed to the best of our abilities and knowledge at the time. Did we really need a chopping board, tyre irons, flip flops, and more than three pairs of socks each? We simply didn't know.

Talking about the chopping board, one of the most important parts of our mobile home was the kitchen. If we were to stay healthy and happy, we had to eat well. Packets of noodles and tinned food had never been our choice of travel food. Because of that, a significant part of our motorcycle luggage was related to food and cooking.

Our kitchen included something like twenty different types of spices, a stash of fresh onions, garlic and ginger. It might sound like a ridiculous amount, but for us they were some of the most important things we were carrying. Using a bag of red lentils, a dash of spices, onion, fresh ginger and garlic, all of which we had in our mobile kitchen, we could cook a deliciously warming Indian dhal in about twenty minutes.

The biggest problem was going to be water. We could carry one or two 1.5L bottles with us but no more. From past experience we knew that for cooking, washing and drinking we ideally needed 5L of water each evening (3L would be enough but we would have to be very careful). We figured out that the only way around it was to buy a large bottle just before camping. This way we wouldn't have to carry all that extra weight around with us all day.

For cooking we bought a multi-fuel stove, with the intention of running it on petrol. I chose it carefully as we needed one that would allow simmering. We also packed one frying pan, two small saucepans which doubled as drinking cups, the already mentioned chopping board, vegetable peeler, a small grater and a few other small items.

When camping we liked to start each day with a freshly brewed cup of coffee and bowl of piping hot porridge, mixed with bananas, cinnamon and raisins. Our diet had to be tasty and healthy. There was no compromise for us when it came to food.

Hitting the road

It was late summer when we decided to leave. We set our departure date for the end of October. We knew it wasn't the best timing, but we didn't want to spend another six months in Poland waiting for spring to arrive. Leaving so late, it was inevitable that winter would eventually catch up with us, but at least we'd be someplace else.

Hitting the road became priority number one, finding a solid base came a close second. Paying to stay in hotels for many months, until the weather improved, was out of the question, and so was staying in a tent. We began looking for ways around it, ideally to stay in places for free. That's how we came across the idea of work exchange. We thought about it and agreed that we wouldn't mind working a few hours a day in exchange for food and accommodation. It seemed like it could be fun and at the same time we hoped we'd learn something useful.

Weeks before leaving we joined one of the largest work exchange websites, Work Away, and almost immediately found something suitable for us. There was a British family living in Greece who needed help on their olive farm. They were flexible with the length of stay, as there was enough work to keep us busy for months. We grabbed the opportunity with both hands and agreed to stay there until spring. It was a good start; an adventure that wouldn't cost us anything. The winter was sorted.

The only downside was that suddenly we had a deadline. We had to agree to arrive on a certain date. The farm owners were going on holiday and needed us at least one day before their departure so they could show us the ropes. We had to get all the way to Greece within just two weeks of leaving Poland. That was very fast for us, much faster than we wanted. Ideally we'd have liked to take at least two months for such a journey, but we had to compromise. We didn't want to miss out on the work exchange opportunity.

Past Greece, we didn't yet have a plan. We had a vague idea though; to drive slowly east until we reached Vladivostok. From there we could go to Japan or South Korea, maybe even to Canada. It would take us at least another two or three years to get all the way across Russia, so in the meantime, it mattered more to focus on our next step. Anyway, we were going to have plenty of time on the farm to think it through.

We left Poland on a grey rainy day. I remember Rebecca wanting to have a picture of our departure and me being stressed out about handling the bike. Wanting to keep her happy, I stopped right outside our old apartment and handed over our camera to some stranger. He looked at us as if we weren't right in the head. To be honest, he had every reason to think this way. The weather was miserable and we were going out on a motorcycle. Wrapped up in multiple layers of clothing, we must have resembled the Michelin man rather than serious adventurers. To add to that, the motorcycle was so overloaded that it looked like an abused donkey; it could barely stay upright. The guy politely took a couple of pictures and said nothing, but his eyes gave away what he was thinking.

The first few miles were a true nightmare. The bike was too heavy to handle. Against common sense and basic motorcycle travel advice, it was the first time we'd driven with such a full load. Each time we stopped at traffic lights, I had difficulty keeping a firm grip of the bike. Luckily it was a quiet Saturday morning and there wasn't much traffic around. I drove slowly and in the end I somehow managed to get us out of the city without any mishaps. It took me some time before I learned how to handle the bike confidently.

We spent our first days trying to escape rain clouds, unsuccessfully. The weather was terrible. But at least we had a chance to test our waterproofs. After many hours spent in one downpour, we realised that the waterproof-ness of our gear was pretty much non-existent. Water was getting in from everywhere; through our shoes, trousers, jackets and helmets. After the second day we covered our boots with duck tape to keep the water out. If I'd thought of it before, I would have bought black tape, more stylish, but instead we turned our footwear luminous silver. It looked like we were wearing space boots. The only piece of gear that was keeping us dry was our gloves. These weren't ordinary gloves. In order to save on unnecessary weight and expense, we bought two pairs of extra large washing-up gloves. We put them on top of our summer protective ones whenever it rained. They were bright green and made our hands hot and sweaty, but they gave us what the other "specialist" motorcycle gear couldn't; they protected us from rain. Luckily fashion was the least of our concerns.

We drove through Czech Republic and Hungary as quickly as possible, almost on autopilot. The objective was simple; to get to dry land. A few days after leaving home we entered Serbia. For us it was a nice change; the culture was different, food prices dropped significantly and people seemed open. There were fewer motorcycles on the roads and we began to attract attention. Unfortunately, the weather was still gloomy. Most of our second day in Serbia was spent driving in heavy rain and wind. Despite this, we enjoyed every single moment. We were battered by the elements, yet for the first time we felt like we were on our adventure. It was nice to see that we were getting used to living with mild discomfort and were slowly adjusting to our new simplistic lifestyle of living on the road.

The weather was awful, but the Serbian scenery was the exact opposite. The country far exceeded our expectations. This lifted our spirits. Driving on Serbian roads was fun too. We were slowly but patiently making our way through the mountainous and lush land. By the end of our first day, soaked and tired, we arrived in a small post-communist village at the top of a mountain. We prayed that there was a hotel or a guesthouse. There was no question of camping that night. It was getting dark and we just wanted a dry bed and a place to rest, no hassle.

The main road was lifeless, probably because it was already pretty dark and had been raining all day. Despite that, we soon realised that the village dogs were on their guard and were not going to waste the opportunity of chasing a couple of newcomers around the place. There were more than a dozen of them. The second they spotted us, all of them came bounding along in our direction. I reacted in a moment of panic by hitting the throttle hard. The front wheel shot off in its own direction. I almost lost control of the bike, but somehow managed to keep it from falling. After regaining balance, I looked back; the angry mob was still after us, but without their biggest advantage, surprise, it turned into nothing more than noise.

We finally made it to a hotel. It was like harking back to the glorious days of communism, with paintings and sculptures of communist heroes, all controversial in their own way. The owners were definitely missing the olden days. Everything about this place belonged to the past, including the receptionist and the decor, which had both seen better days. That said, we liked the place. It was different, warm, had bags of character and most importantly, there was a room waiting for us. The room itself was very basic, with two separate beds covered with old red blankets. The air was stale and furniture pretty non-existent, except a large soviet propaganda painting hanging on the wall in the middle of our room. The place was great.

Wet to the bone, we dropped our gear in a corner and headed straight back to the restaurant for a cup of something hot. We weren't hungry but wanted something to warm our bodies. Not caring about our looks, we wore only our thermals base layers, socks and woollen hats. We were cold and, besides, everything else was soaked through. The minute we showed up in the hall, the old lady from reception ran toward us. It seemed she wasn't impressed by the sight of us. It hit us that maybe our style was too casual for the establishment, but it wasn't that. She immediately ordered us to put on some old slippers and a moment later brought extra blankets to wrap around us. She wasn't concerned about the way we looked but about our wellbeing. Surprised but glad to be taken care of, we did as we were told. After a short wait, hot chocolate arrived and it was simply divine. We figured out that it was probably because it was made with fresh milk straight from a cow's tit. We slept like logs that night. That was exactly what we needed.

The next day we left early and drove towards the border. We wished we had more time to spend in Serbia and for a moment regretted that we'd agreed to do a farm-sit in Greece, but we promised ourselves that we'd return to Serbia one day.

Ballooning dogs

"It's a strange world. Let's keep it that way."

by Warren Ellis

The climate changed as we drove through Albania; it finally became dry and sunny. We were glad we didn't have to worry about the rain anymore. In fact it suddenly became so hot that we had to take quite a few layers off.

Along with the weather, the landscape changed. In comparison to Serbia, it was flatter and much less varied. Also there was something about Albania that made us feel as if we were stepping into a film set of a spaghetti western. One thing that was bizarre, were all the dead dogs by the side of the roads. It wasn't just the fact they were dead and in high numbers, but that nobody seemed to do anything about them. Having lain there, for lord knows how long, in the scorching sun, their bodies were puffed up like balloons, all four legs up in the air. It looked like they may explode at any moment.

On top of that the whole country seemed kind of deserted. Roads were quiet, at one point we found ourselves on a short stretch of motorway with no other vehicles in eyesight. For a moment we wondered if we were supposed to be there, until we spotted a traffic cop. It seemed like an unusual sight, until we realised that traffic police is ever-present in Albania. I just hoped they wouldn't stop us. I had mixed feelings about the Albanian police. On the one hand, it was pretty reassuring to see their presence, which indeed seemed to work, as most drivers kept their speed in check, but on the other hand, I was concerned that two tourists on a motorcycle, looking strangely out of place, could seem like a lucrative catch for a traffic cop. I was worried that they could try to hustle us for a bribe.

With that in mind, I tried really hard to stay within the speed limit. But by the end of the second day, I was becoming tired of driving slowly on empty roads. Once, after completing a long and slow climb for hours up a winding mountain road and finally reaching the top, ahead of us appeared this perfectly straight stretch of road descending as far as we could see. Excitement got the better of me and I allowed myself to gain speed. I wasn't driving very fast, but it didn't matter. It was enough to get us in trouble. At the bottom of the road, hidden behind a bush, the police was waiting. I got pulled over. They knew exactly where to position themselves and I fell straight into their trap.

A grumpy looking policeman approached our motorcycle and showed us the reading on his radar. I knew it was right and there was nothing to debate about. The crime had been committed and the punishment was to follow. He avoided talking or even looking at us, as if any emotional connection would weaken his authority. In a cold and official manner he asked for a passport. I hesitated for a moment. By giving it to him, I would become completely at his mercy. Unfortunately, there was no other choice. With my passport in his hand, the policeman disappeared in his car and we were left waiting by the side of the road. He was gone for over twenty minutes. During that time we anxiously tried to evaluate our situation. We almost expected that upon his return we'd be asked to pay a bribe. Soon enough everything became clear when the cop returned with a ticket. There was no negotiation, no talking, he just handed it over. The amount was already filled in. Luckily it was relatively small. With broken English and hand gestures, he explained that he'd keep my document until we returned with receipt of payment. That didn't sound good. We didn't want to leave the passport behind. Besides we didn't even really know where to go or what to do. It was already late afternoon and we expected that it could take hours before our return. When we asked for more information, he just pointed his hand and said assertively "Bank". We jumped on the bike and followed his simple direction. Within ten minutes we found a town with a small bank. After queuing for half an hour, we were able to pay the fine. With the receipt in hand we drove back. I really hoped that the police car was still there. It would have been a disaster if it wasn't. Luckily it was. The cop was still as official and unemotional as before, but I got my passport back and off we went.

We were surprised how straightforward and organised the whole situation had been. Not wanting any more adventures like this, I promised not to speed anymore, and I kept my promise, for a while at least.

Free lunch

"There's no such thing as a free lunch"

by Milton Friedman

We arrived at the farm one day before the agreed deadline. The timing was ideal as it allowed us to get familiar with the area, learn about the farm and spend a little time with the owners before they went on holiday. They seemed friendly and we liked being around them. We also liked the farm. There wasn't much time for the handover, but luckily there wasn't much to learn either. Everything seemed simple enough and the instructions were good. Before we even realised it, it was just the two of us, plus a bunch of animals.

The first day we discovered that there was very little work to be done. Between the two of us, it took less than ten minutes in the morning and even less in the evening. That's because the farm was pretty small; it consisted of only a couple of pigs, some sheep, a handful of poultry and a smelly old dog. We enjoyed being around the animals. I wasn't too fond of the pigs but they charmed Rebecca after a couple of days. Feeding them became her chore.

We quickly got used to our daily routine and found farm sitting easy and enjoyable. The atmosphere was relaxed. In our spare time we explored the area, chilled in the hammock and read books. We were our own bosses and could do whatever we liked. As for our accommodation, the owners had a beautiful big house, which they rented out in the main tourist season, but during their absence we were allowed to stay in it. It was surrounded by hundreds of olive trees. We were living comfortably, in the heart of the Peloponnese, only ten minutes away from the sea.

The hens laid us fresh eggs every day, we baked our own bread and there was a large garden supplying us with fresh vegetables. We had everything we needed. The first three weeks on the farm were real fun and it didn't feel like work at all. It was more like a holiday. Life was good for us, but we knew that soon enough we'd have to earn our keep and we were ready for that.

As expected, everything changed when the owners returned. We were downgraded to a smaller house, which was a basically a self-built shack. It was cold at night, hot during the day and there was no hot water. The owners, John and Sally, were from England and had been living in Greece for around fifteen years. They'd learned the language and become part of the community. They immediately took over the animal chores, which was something we'd actually really enjoyed and were a bit gutted to lose. On the second day we started our work exchange. The holiday was over; the work began. The arrangement was simple; we were to work five hours a day, five days a week in exchange for food and lodging. Five hours didn't sound like a lot until we started our first big task; digging holes for grow beds. The soil was hardened by the sun so the task required a lot of effort. The one good thing was that we weren't just assigned to the task and left to it, but actually worked together with the owners.

Living and working with a British family, it quickly dawned on us that except for the location, there was nothing Greek about the farm. At times it felt almost as if we were living in England.

Our food arrangement also changed. We were no longer our own bosses. To get on, we had to conform. As for breakfast and lunch, we were asked to join the family in their house. At the beginning we liked that they wanted to include us and share their food, but soon we realised that it wasn't such a good thing. Their breakfast consisted of a piece of toast and a cup of tea. For us breakfast is the most important meal of the day and we like to fill our bellies with something tasty and healthy to set us up for the day ahead. Their breakfast didn't work for us. We didn't feel comfortable enough in their company to ask for more, but it wasn't possible for us to go on like this. After a few days of eating a single slice of toast for breakfast we'd had enough. We talked to John and Sally and together we found a solution. From that day on we were given our own food to prepare in the mornings. This new arrangement worked for everyone. It meant we got to eat as much as we wanted and it allowed us time to slowly wake up before meeting for work.

When it came to the main meal, unfortunately there wasn't such an easy solution as there had been with breakfasts. Part of the work exchange agreement was that we would be given three meals a day. We'd already opted to prepare breakfast ourselves, but didn't want to prepare all the meals ourselves. It wasn't an option. We'd have to accept what we were given. The problem was that their cooking didn't suit us very well. John and Sally loved their meat and it was the main ingredient of every meal. We, on the other hand, prefer vegetables and more varied cuisine. Meat is not our typical food choice. Even if it was, not many people can stomach sausages and minced meat every day. Regardless, we always appreciated what we were given and ate gratefully without complaining. Secretly, we longed for our own cooking.

To make matters worse, soon the relationship with John and Sally started to change. We began noticing that we were being treated as cheap labour. For them the exchange was strictly a business transaction and John was pretty open about it. When it rained it was impossible to work outdoors, but the time wasn't wasted; we used it preparing food to be frozen, ready for the days of hardcore olive picking that lay ahead. John though, saw these days as a waste of our work time. He had a sarcastic sense of humour and would joke that "today we wouldn't eat because we hadn't earned it". He joked (in that very English way that isn't actually a joke at all) that we were "cheaper than Bangladeshi workers" who were often taken on by local farmers to work for a pittance. This attitude started rubbing on us. For us the idea of work exchange was different. Though being important, it wasn't just about saving money. Primarily it was about a fair exchange, new experiences, fun and learning. We came to the farm with a romantic image of picking olives in Greece, but that was slowly being destroyed. We never avoided hard work or getting our hands dirty, but in return we wanted to be well fed and appreciated. John's motion of "earning our food" was short of offensive, mainly because it was very unfair. The two of us working on the sub-minimum wage would in a single day earn enough to pay for a week's worth of food; good, decent food. In any case, we were giving much more than we were actually receiving.

Regardless of a few uncomfortable moments, we still wanted to experience olive picking. That was why we were there.

Once olive picking starts, all olives have to be collected as quickly as possible, ideally within a few days. For us it meant that we'd have to work from early morning all the way to dusk, even up to twelve hours a day. To offset these extra hours, not long before the picking started, we were told that we could have a one week holiday if we wanted. But then, when we actually decided to take them up on the offer, Sally and John seemed pissed off with us, as if we were taking something away from them. They were strange people.

Greek holidays

For our one-week holiday destination we chose Santorini, a dream-like Greek island. It seemed a nice place to spend our few precious days alone. We needed it; we had to escape somewhere nice. It was simply vital for our sanity. We wanted, once again, to taste freedom and adventure, even if only for a short time. To get there, we had to first drive to Athens. Before catching a ferry, we decided to spend some time in the capital. Driving all the way there and not seeing it wouldn't have been right.

Through CouchSurfing Rebecca found a local person to stay with. We'd been pretty isolated living on the farm and now wanted to socialise, have fun and finally meet some Greeks. It was exciting and almost felt like I'd imagine the first day out of prison.

We didn't waste time and drove straight to our host. Nektarios was living in the heart of the city, in a small but cosy apartment. He was a friendly guy with a wicked sense of humour. For instance, shortly after our arrival Rebecca politely asked if she could use the toilet; the reply was an abrupt "No". He tried to keep a straight face, but his friendly eyes gave him away. Apparently it was a silly question; of course she could use the toilet. After that, we made ourselves at home. With Nektarios, there wasn't much ice to break.

We didn't know before arriving, but it was our host's birthday. We wanted to meet local people and our wish quickly became reality; the first evening in Athens we were invited to a birthday party. It was in a Greek restaurant, with traditional food and live music playing in the background. There were about twenty of us; Nektarios's friends and family. They were all very welcoming and the atmosphere couldn't have been better. Soon after we'd arrived, the table started filling up with delicious food and drinks. There was plenty for everyone. We ate, drank and talked for hours. It was an evening filled with fun and laughter. We were thrilled.

The next morning we woke up early, as Nektarios was leaving for work. He agreed to join us in the afternoon. We had the whole morning to ourselves and decided to use the time to explore the old city. It was within easy walking distance from the apartment. Once we got there, we discovered that the place was packed with people. As we strolled around, we understood why; it was simply charming. Trendy cafés and restaurants were seamlessly blended together with ancient ruins and historical sites. Open spaces were turned into a temporary stage where street performers of all ages bravely tried to entertain hard-to-impress crowds. The old town attracted locals and tourists alike.

Later that day we were joined by Nektarios. Together we went on a tour of the Parthenon. We couldn't have hoped for a better guide; he was passionate about Athens and everything Greek, and we could tell how proud it made him showing us the country's cultural heritage. We finished our tour in a nearby cafe. Tired from walking, we sat on the patio, looking at people passing by, drinking strong coffee and enjoying the gentle warmth of the evening sun.

After a couple of exceptionally good days in Athens, we resumed travelling. Our holiday was only short and if we were to see Santorini, we had to get on a ferry. It was time to move on. We got on the motorcycle early in the morning, just after six, hopeful that we could avoid the worst of the city's traffic. It was in vain. The route to Piraeus, the largest port in Greece, was overflowing with cars and motorcycles. A mere ten miles took us over an hour to cover. It was almost like playing Dodgems; chaos and narrow escapes throughout. By luck or some other supernatural power (certainly not just by skill) we managed to make it in one piece to a ferry ticket office and bought three tickets for Santorini; two for us and one for the motorcycle.

The next step was to find the right ferry, which wasn't too difficult. Once there, we joined others waiting. There was no queue, but a semi-circle of people, cars and bikes, all pushing inwards. The single person responsible for controlling the boarding stood no chance against the crowd. There were no rules. After a few hours of waiting and negotiating for the best position, they opened the gates and everyone poured in, all at once. It was organised chaos. Everyone wanted to be first. Having a motorcycle, not a car, was a big advantage as it allowed us to squeeze through with other bikes and quickly get inside. We were directed to a designated motorcycle parking area. There was plenty of space for the bike. Once in place, Rebecca slowly began unpacking the bike, while I tried to figure out the best way to secure it. I knew that throughout the night it would have to withstand some serious rocking at sea and the last thing I wanted was to find the bike toppled over in the morning. I had some ropes with me and used them to fasten the bike as best as I could, but I wasn't sure it was enough. Soon an attendant came over. He didn't seem concerned and quickly attached the motorcycle for us, using his own fasteners. My enthusiasm couldn't match his experience; after less than a minute the bike was safe. Free to go, we went looking for somewhere comfortable for the voyage.

The first half an hour on the ferry took strategy. It seemed that very few people had paid for a cabin so for the rest, boarding became a race to get the most comfortable spot. That spot, once taken, was guarded for the whole journey. It was probably especially important because we were travelling during the night; it meant the difference between getting some sleep or none at all. Restaurants seemed to be some of the most luxurious spots. They offered comfortably padded sofas, but the downside was that customers were expected to spend money on overpriced and tasteless food. I suppose there's always a choice; pay for a cabin, pay for food, or sleep on the floor. It's a big money making machine. We wanted to fit in, but it didn't really work for us. First we tried the floor, but found it uncomfortable, so after midnight we shifted to the restaurant. It was a bold move, because we definitely weren't going to buy anything. It took us almost an hour to find a suitable spot. By then the staff wasn't bothered anymore. We stayed there for the rest of the voyage.

It was still the middle of the night when we reached our destination. We were shattered. Unloading didn't take long, though. We took the fastest available route to our CouchSurfing host, as we badly needed a sleep. It wasn't even 4 a.m. when we arrived there. John, our host, had previously assured us that we should come at whatever time we reached the island, but still, it felt a bit uncomfortable waking him up so early. To our surprise, he came out with a big smile and welcomed us to his house. John was actually named Yannis, but preferred to be called by the English equivalent. He was a heavy-metal-loving web designer from Greece, who spent his spare time mastering the art of Japanese sword fighting. Even though he was born in Thessaloniki, he possessed a great deal of information about Santorini and was happy to share it with us. He also shared his coffee, which helped us stay awake the first couple of hours at his place. At dawn we couldn't stay awake anymore and went to sleep on John's sofa.

We were really happy that we connected with John so easily, but there was one thing that we just couldn't get over; the sofa was unbearable to sleep on. One, it was way too narrow for both of us. Two, the mattress was paper thin (almost like our camping mat). Three, some of the wooden slats beneath the mattress were missing and the few left were digging into our bodies. After around twenty four hours of travelling we expected to sleep like logs on pretty much anything, but that wasn't the case on John's sofa. We failed to get any rest. It was very unfortunate because John was a fantastic guy and we enjoyed his company, but there was no way we could have stayed there another night. We decided to find some other place to sleep and to come back to John's in a couple of days to hang out and cook together. We left later that morning.

The previous few weeks on the farm had been really good for our budget. We'd spent next to nothing, and now decided it was time to treat ourselves. It was nice to discover that our negotiating position was very good. There were hardly any tourists, so most hotels offered as much as seventy percent off their standard price. Within two hours of searching, comparing and negotiating, we found our dream place in the city of Fira. This traditional Greek house had our name written all over it. After some friendly haggling with the owner, we came to a very reasonable agreement and quickly moved in. It was like stepping into a postcard.

For the most part of the year, the city becomes a tourist magnet, but there is a good reason for that; Fira is delightful. All houses look alike, but precisely that makes the city so unique. The city, being painted white and blue, magnifies the brightness of the sun and highlights the deep colours of the sea. Built on a steep hill, Fira proudly stretches way above the sea line. Yet on both sides it's dramatically encapsulated by vertical rock. Amongst the houses, there are hundreds of small chapels scattered around. They make Fira even more special.

We later learned that these chapels were built not purely for the love of God, but as a clever way to avoid paying taxes. Greeks' sense of creativity never ceases to amaze us.

Our house wasn't different from the rest; it was an old cottage, painted snow white, with blue frames around the windows and doors. There was no chapel attached to it, but it didn't matter as there was one just opposite our front door. To complete the Santorini postcard, occasionally donkeys passed by just outside our windows. We felt like we were in a dream, our Greek dream. But there is even more to Santorini than meets the eye. The island is filled with hidden treasures, surprises and unique tastes. Being created by a volcano, Santorini owes its inherent nature to violent eruptions. The volcano is still active and remains both a blessing and a curse. The most recent eruption happened only in the twentieth century so the threat of it happening again is pretty real.

Volcanic ash and rock cover the entire surface of the island, but that's actually a blessing; fruits and vegetables find this mineral-rich soil to be a perfect ground for thriving. Because of that, Santorini is famed for delicious tomatoes, aubergines and grapes, amongst other things. There are some really unique beaches there, too; the red one was our favourite.

Our time on the island flew by. We enjoyed every single moment and weren't looking forward to going back to the farm. Travelling and visiting Santorini was a different world; a world of adventures and discovery.

Freedom regained

On our way back we stopped over in Athens. We wanted to visit Nektarios and give him a small present from Santorini; a bottle of local wine. When unpacking the motorcycle, unfortunately the bottle fell out on the street and smashed. The wine ended up all over our clothes. As a result we came to Nektarios stinking of alcohol. It was good we'd already met, otherwise he probably wouldn't have let us in. We stayed overnight, delaying our return to the farm.

Our short trip had finally come to an end. These few days offered us a taste of adventure and also made us realise how much we were missing. Now we wanted more. New ideas and plans began sprouting in our heads, and these made returning to work a real challenge. We had little motivation for the farm work. Probably the only thing that brought us back there was the prospect of olive picking. It was something that we definitely wanted to experience and we were actually looking forward to it. Everything was ready when we got back. The olives were ripe enough and waiting to be picked. We sprang to work the morning after our return.

The work was harder than we'd expected, but it was also great fun. Olive picking is simple, but pretty labour intensive and time consuming. It starts off with spreading special netting under the first chosen tree. Then somebody goes up that tree and cuts the most fruitful branches with a chainsaw. Others work on the ground. There's plenty of work for everyone. To make work easier, there are a few specialist tools to choose from, all designed basically to separate olives from the olive branches. It takes a few hours to process one tree. We worked like this twelve hours straight, from dusk until dawn, day in day out; with only short breaks for sustenance. A few days were enough to squeeze any romantic notions out of our sore bodies. The fun factor was disappearing quickly, and without it, work was getting even more strenuous.

As if the work wasn't hard enough, we noticed that Sally and John often skilfully and subtly avoided doing the hardest jobs. There was one particular job on the ground that I got stuck with. We called it "working with Dino". Dino was a brand name for a large machine used to process large olive branches. It was very efficient, but required a lot of strength to operate. Dino vibrated like crazy (even more than my motorcycle) and would often shoot back with olive bullets. The impact was painful and bruising, almost like a close shot with a paintball. I didn't want Rebecca to work on Dino and for obvious reasons Sally avoided it like the plague. John spent a lot of time up trees with his chainsaw, so Dino was all mine.

On the fourth day we drove to the processing plant, where olives were turned into raw oil. It was probably the most satisfying task in days. Seeing tones of olives going in one end of the machine and oil flowing out the other was worth those days of hard work. By the end of the evening we returned home with our own olive oil, completely organic and pure. We were happy, but also tired and very hungry. As usual, we sat by the table, waiting to be served food. Then came doughnuts. Apparently that's what they make every year with their newly pressed batch of olive oil. We politely ate two each and left plenty of room for a proper meal. But it never came. We couldn't believe it; after slaving away for twelve hours in the scorching heat, in return we get junk food, freaking doughnuts! We can take a fair amount of crap from people, and we did from John, but we take our food very seriously. It was the final straw; we were done with this place.

We kept our word and stayed for another two days to finish off the olive picking. There were fewer olives then expected that season, so the atmosphere was sombre. Less olives meant less work, which was good news for us but not so good for Sally and John. We were counting down the days till the end. Not long before we'd finished, John and Sally decided to offer our labour to their neighbours. Who knows, maybe we ate too many doughnuts and they needed to get their money's worth. But by then it didn't really matter. We were leaving. The first morning after our job was done, we packed the motorcycle and off we went.

We learned a lot from the experience. Surely, there were ups and downs, but still, we were glad we'd done it. When leaving, we felt reassured knowing that there's always a way to continue our journey even on the smallest of budgets.

Getting stuck

The winter was almost upon us and ferries were soon to stop their services to some destinations. A few hundred miles north it was already cold and there was risk of it snowing at any time. For us it meant that going north was not an option. So we figured that our best bet was the south of Turkey. On our way there we hoped to visit some Greek islands.

Being back on the road felt really nice; with the wind on our side, we looked forward to our new adventures. Finally we had no deadlines and no set destination. We drove slowly and stopped often. There was no rush to be anywhere.

The first day after leaving the farm we drove along the coast and later spent the night on a sandy beach. It was so warm that we slept under the stars without bothering to put our tent up. In the morning we continued wandering about. For the second night we found a field situated near the sea. To get there we had to go across a stony beach. It was only a short drive, so without a second's thought I went ahead. The momentum kept us going for a while, but it wasn't enough. Soon the stones slowed the bike down and eventually brought it to a halt. Rebecca got off to give me a push, but the bike was only getting more stuck, each moment deeper and deeper, until it was sitting on its belly, half of the back wheel buried under stones and sand. The more effort I made, the deeper the bike sank. There was no panic though; we were almost exactly where we wanted to be, just around fifty yards away from our chosen camping spot. We slowly unpacked the bike, partly to make it lighter, partly to camp out. Rebecca went to pitch our tent, whilst I stayed with the bike. I knew that moving it wasn't going to be easy. After all, it was almost four hundred pounds in weight; much more than I could carry in my hands. One by one, I tried everything I could think of; digging around it, putting things under the wheel for better traction, rocking the bike back and forth to build momentum, even dropping the bike to the side to pull it out. Nothing made any significant difference. The motorcycle wasn't going anywhere and there was absolutely nobody around to give us a hand. At least I had plenty of time at hand. After over two hours of trying to force the bike out, I thought of another solution. It occurred to me that I could remove some air from the back tyre to widen the grip. It worked like magic. Within minutes the bike was out of the hole and moving slowly towards harder terrain.

We could finally enjoy our camping spot, which was absolutely worth the trouble. The place was stunning and completely isolated. We would have stayed there for another few days, but didn't have enough food. We had to move on in the morning.

The next day we arrived in Athens and drove straight to the ferry port. We were about to buy our tickets when I noticed that one of our passports was missing. We looked at each other and ran back to the motorcycle. Without saying a word, we began the search. The good thing about living on a motorcycle is that there aren't too many places to store things. We frantically looked through every thread of clothing, at least a few times, even opened up our tent to check the inside pocket, but couldn't find it there either. We had no idea where it was, but knew for certain that it wasn't with us. We were stuck. There was nothing else we could do, so we just sat next to the bike, thinking through our options. The passport was vital to continue our journey into Turkey. The only solution was to find the embassy and apply for a new one. It was to be a costly mistake, but there was no other choice. The situation was far from ideal. I felt annoyed and guilty. Usually, I'm the one in charge of our passports, so I felt responsible for misplacing it. If only I could remember where I'd left it, but I couldn't, at least not at that moment. After calming down a bit, it came to me, I realised where the passport was. It dawned on me that I'd left it in Santorini. I remembered that when we'd booked into our dream accommodation the owner took one of our passports as a security deposit. With this new information, we rushed to the nearest McDonalds to get online. Once we'd got the phone number off the internet, I called the hotel. The owner answered after the first ring. His English was pretty bad, but he understood me well enough. He knew exactly why I was calling. The passport was there and it was safe. The panic was over. We arranged for the passport to be sent to our next destination. There was no need for us to stay in Athens any longer so I used my national ID to book the next ferry. Our next stop was the island of Chios.

Local customs

We arrived in Chios late afternoon. Right away we noticed that the island was much more tranquil than Santorini, with just a handful of tourists, barely visible around main cities and beaches. It's an enchanting little island, located just off the coast of Turkey. For us it was a jumping off point for Asia, a gateway to another continent. The only thing we needed was my passport.

Soon after arriving we booked into our hotel, a short drive outside the main town. The place was almost empty because it was out of season. The owner was very friendly and didn't mind when we informed him that we were expecting a delivery. Chios is small, so we had plenty of time to see most of it.

One of the highlights of our visit was a small village called Pyrgi. For us it was just the epitome of Greek culture. It was exactly as we'd imagined Greece to be. In fact, it was one of very few places in the country where traditional ways of living seemed preserved. Going to Pyrgi felt like travelling back in time. We slowly strolled through the narrow streets, immersed in their charm. Houses existed almost as pieces of art. They were competing for attention and asking for admiration at the same time. Even the cherry tomatoes hanging outside houses looked more like part of a creative installation than simply a practical way to sun dry them. Traditionally dressed men with moustaches talked rowdily and smoked cigars. Fishermen with their skin and hair relentlessly beaten by the elements prepared their nets for their next sea venture. Next to them, cats did what cats do best; lazed in the shade, patiently waiting for evening to come.

As we continued deeper into the village, we started noticing something curious. Time after time we came across an old lady, or a group of them, sitting right outside their houses, engaged in some unfamiliar activity. They were all wearing black. Soon we realised that they were cleaning mastic, a product for which Pyrgi is renowned. Mastic is used everywhere on the island and is probably the most popular souvenir item in shops. It's used for infusing alcohol, for sweets, snacks, chewing gum, even as an ingredient for cooking. Later we learned that mastic is obtained from the mastic tree in small droplets resembling tears, hence it being known as "tears of Chios". Interestingly, mastic has been used for treating ailments since ancient times and is still used in traditional folk medicine. What's more, in Greece, it was once even given as a remedy for snakebites.

It was our greatest luck that we came to Pyrgi at the right time. Mastic had just been collected and needed cleaning. It's a straightforward task of removing small bits of tree bark from the rest. It's all done by hand with a small knife. More than being hard work, the process is time consuming and repetitive.

At one point during our stroll around the meandering streets, Rebecca approached one of the elderly ladies. I thought she just wanted a closer look, but to my surprise she asked if she could help. The lady agreed, happy to gain some company. She was probably in her eighties. Her face was kind, but wore signs of hard work. She showed Rebecca what needed to be done and within minutes they both set about the task in hand. Rebecca sat with her for almost an hour, trying to copy the moves. Though seemingly simple, the task required skill. In contrast to Rebecca's clumsy hand movements, the lady looked as if she could do it with her eyes closed. She was a chatty old lady. Some things we understood, most we didn't, but she was happy to have somebody to listen to her. That seemed to be what Pyrgi ladies did as they worked with the mastic; they gossiped themselves out of boredom.

Visiting Chios was a perfect way to say goodbye to Greece. Finally, when my passport showed up, it was time for a new chapter. Turkey was only ten miles away and we couldn't wait to cross over and leave the European Union.

We arrived in Turkey by ferry. The journey only took half an hour and after unloading the bike we headed straight for border control. We found the customs office and joined the queue. The building was small and most people were let through quickly, partly because there weren't any tourists. When it was finally our turn, we approached one of the customs officers and showed our documents. He looked at them and, to our surprise, sent us away with a finger pointing to the side of the building. We were ordered to wait. No explanation was given, so we just did as we'd been told.

About twenty minutes later some guy came to us. He had a carefully trimmed moustache that made him look older than he was, and wore a plain grey sweater under a black leather jacket. On his neck hung a makeshift identification badge, which only made him look more suspicious. Without explaining anything, he asked for our passports. Alarm bells rang in our heads. I ran back to the customs desk for advice and was told to hand over our documents to the stranger in the leather jacket. It was all unnerving, but we followed the instructions. He took our passports and disappeared.

We waited for a long time; long enough to get seriously worried that we had just made a pretty big mistake and lost our passports. Luckily, he returned. Then our passports changed hands and went back to the customs officer, the one that had sent us away in the first place. As we approached the desk, the moustached guy asked us for money. Only then we realised that he was an agent, not a secret agent but one selling mandatory vehicle insurance. Once we'd paid the set fee, we got our documents back.

But the process wasn't over yet. Next we were told to go outside to our vehicle and wait. About ten minutes later another officer came. His task was to search our bike, but first he thoroughly looked through our passports. He checked every single page in each document, then with utmost seriousness pointed at a couple of entry stamps from South America and asked if we had any drugs with us. We weren't sure whether he was joking or not, but laughed anyway and affirmed that we didn't. Then we were asked to open our luggage. Initially he starting looking as thoroughly as he had done through our passports, but after a few minutes he got bored and gave up. We were at last allowed into Turkey.

Without doubt it was the strangest border crossing we'd ever experienced.

First impressions

Our first destination in Turkey was Cesme; a town on the western coast. It was only half an hour away from the port so we got there early in the morning. We liked it from the start. It's a small atmospheric place. It was quiet, almost deserted, when we arrived. Though it was off season, it was hard for us to find a hotel within our budget. The place was overpriced and nobody was willing to negotiate.

Finally, not too far from the centre, we discovered a little family run boutique hotel with vacant rooms. There were no other guests and the owner was happy to come down with the price quite a bit. It was still early, not later than seven in the morning when we moved in with all our gear. The family was in the middle of their breakfast. Once we'd settled in, they invited us for some tea and a snack. We ended up having our first ever full Turkish breakfast. And it wasn't just any breakfast; it was a typical local morning feast.

It didn't take long before we knew the whole family. They were very welcoming, both to their house and their country. It was a very pleasant start to our Turkish adventure. After breakfast and settling into our room, we went for a morning stroll around the town. We could tell that a lot of hard work was put into making Cesme look beautiful. We especially liked seeing all the small finishing touches; handmade pieces of art appearing in the most unexpected places, waiting to be discovered. The town was oozing with character.

Everywhere we looked, there were hotels and restaurants, ready to welcome hordes of tourists in season. The town was the first place we'd visited in Turkey, but we suspected it was a real gem. Later our suspicions proved true.

After a couple of days, eager to discover more of Turkey, we left Cesme. We were really touched to see that the family came out to wish us farewell. In the final minute, the mother took her daughter's scarf off her and put it around Rebecca's neck to keep her warm (even the daughter was surprised by this gesture). After saying our goodbyes we drove south, along the coast.

Our next stop was the city of Izmir, where we found a CouchSurfing host to stay with for a couple of nights. I didn't know how to get to her house but had written down the address and was confident that we could easily find it, with just a little help from locals.

Getting to Izmir seemed easy enough, but once we got to the city, finding the right address proved anything but easy. We got lost within minutes. Even asking for directions wasn't helping. For about an hour, we were driving round and round in circles, not getting any closer. Somebody would tell us to go one way, only to be sent in the opposite direction by someone else minutes later. It was very frustrating. Then one guy came to our rescue. Instead of telling us where to go, he dropped what he was doing and instructed us to follow his car. To make sure where to go, he called our host to confirm the address. We drove behind him for almost twenty minutes. When we reached the destination, our host was already waiting outside her house. If it wasn't for that guy, we would have probably never found the right address. We were so grateful to have met him. His help and kindness gave us a very positive first impression of the city.

Our host was a young Turkish lady, who worked for an international company and wrote a travel blog in her spare time. She was living on her own in a large three bedroom apartment. Apparently it was a typical size flat. That evening we didn't spend any time together as she'd already arranged to go out with mates to a sold-out gig. We were tired anyway so that worked out well for us.

The following morning, our host left for work and wasn't coming back till the late evening. We were given our own key to come and go as we pleased, but felt that it wasn't the CouchSurfing experience we were really after. Before making any decisions, we went out for the day, exploring the city. We decided that if we liked it, we'd stay, possibly on our own. If we didn't, we'd move on the next morning.

We travelled to the city centre by train and within minutes of arriving, we knew that we wanted to hang around for another few days. We liked Izmir from the start. We decided to move to a hotel, closer to the centre. It was very easy to find a place and the following morning, after thanking our host for her hospitality, we moved.

Izmir, being so vibrant and diverse, captivated us. We found ourselves in the midst of a culture that was almost completely unknown to us, and were hungry to know more about it. We spent long hours around the main square, where people came to socialise, take pictures and feed pigeons. At the heart of the main square was a small, beautifully decorated old mosque that attracted crowds of people. A short walk from the square was the promenade. It stretched forever along the sea. We enjoyed watching young boys looking for muscles attached to a concrete construction. Above all, our biggest fascination in Izmir was the bazaar, which just seemed like the best place to explore the world of Turkish cuisine and the coffee culture.

Getting lost in the vast maze of narrow alleys became our most enjoyable pastime. We were on a culinary quest and tried to sample everything on offer at least once; most food was very tasty, all inexpensive. Only one dish ended up in the bin; cold cows' tongue. I bravely tried it, but for me it was inedible. Rebecca passed on this one. We religiously drank Turkish coffee; a few times a day, every day. We couldn't resist passing by a traditional coffee house and not staying for at least one cup. We spent hours this way; slowly sipping strong coffee, eating sickly sweet baklava, listening to local street musicians and enjoying the hustle and the bustle of the busy bazaar. Once we were done with our coffee, we set off in search of our daily fill of freshly squeezed pomegranate juice. This healthy pleasure cost a mere 50 pence for two cups. As if that wasn't enough, there was a free Balkan music festival right in the middle of the main square. This lively entertainment was just the extra icing on an already delicious cake. Needless to say, we fell in love with Izmir.

Leaving and arriving

After leaving Izmir, we headed east, hoping we could reach Konya while it was still warm enough to drive the motorcycle. We wished to see the whirling dervishes there and to then continue as far east as the weather permitted, maybe even all the way to Cappadocia. There was so much of Turkey that we wanted to see before becoming winter-bound on the south coast.

On the way to Konya we stopped in Pamukkale, a city renowned for its travertines; terraces made from white rock deposited by mineral rich water from hot springs. To our surprise there were only a few other people there. We pretty much had the whole place to ourselves. Once again, surprise surprise, it wasn't the right season for tourists.

As requested at the entrance, we took our shoes off and walked through the terraces barefoot. The hot spring was flowing slowly on the surface and, contrary to what we'd expected, it was cold, so cold that occasionally we found ourselves stepping on thick frozen patches. The ice created a burning sensation on our skin which forced us to jump quickly to a warmer spot, where fresh water had just came out of the ground. We felt like kids playing "Hot and Cold". The whole experience was very special. After a few hours in Pamukkale, the time came to move on. Wanting to connect with somebody local, Rebecca found a CouchSurfing host for us; this time in Denizli, a large city near Pamukkale. We headed there right after our icy hot spring experience.

For once, we found the right address easily. Our new host, Aylin, welcomed us as if we were family or very good friends she hadn't seen for years. She was kind, cheerful and generous She was also a great cook. Spending time in her house with her and her son was a real pleasure. We talked a lot and laughed even more. Aylin became our window into Turkey. We learned so much from her. It was she who told us that in Turkey there's an old custom of cooking halva soon after somebody's death, and saying that you want to eat somebody's halva is like wishing them dead. We learned this peculiar fact exactly as we were eating Aylin's cooked halva. And it was truly delicious.

She also found time to take us to a local bazaar where we bought some fruits and vegetables, some of which we'd never seen before. She told us what things should cost and that it's normal, almost customary, to try fruit before purchasing. We stayed with her for two days and would probably have stayed longer, but the winter was upon us and we had to hit the road. By the time we left Denizli, winter had truly arrived. Temperatures at night dropped way below zero. Days were also getting increasingly cold.

According to the weather forecast, the snow was coming our way. We had to act quickly. Going further east wasn't a good idea anymore; our only option was to head down south instead. There, by the coast, we would be sheltered from the cold. For our next destination we chose Antalya. In this large seaside city we hoped to find a relatively cheap place to stay for a couple of months. But first we had to get there.

The weather wasn't too bad when we left Aylin's, but it deteriorated rapidly. It soon became unbearable for driving on a motorcycle. The winter had eventually caught up with us and we weren't ready for it, not one bit. We tried shielding our bodies with every bit of clothing we had, basically stuffing our jackets and trousers as if it we were Christmas turkeys. It didn't really help, though. The cold was penetrating easily through our unsuitable layers. Wind was the worst, relentlessly blowing away any remaining warmth. We were both shivering uncontrollably. Operating the motorcycle was pretty hard, having lost the feeling in my fingers. The whole experience was exhausting and beyond unpleasant.

Tea breaks were our escape. They were probably the only way to keep our bodies from hypothermia, apart from stopping and booking ourselves into a hotel, of course. Unfortunately they never lasted long enough. Once, during one of these short breaks, I placed my cold motorcycle gloves near the engine to warm them up. It worked a treat. When I returned they were warm and comfortable, a pleasure to wear. It was a luxury I couldn't resist. I kept doing it, even though I noticed that the material was occasionally melting. Unfortunately, three stops further I'd managed to burn a proper hole in them. From that point onwards my fingers were completely unprotected. We continued regardless of the discomfort. We had to. After a long few hours of putting up with the weather, we finally arrived in Antalya. It was a big relief. Now we just had to find a place to live for a month or so.

Antalya was our safe haven; a place where we could lie dormant until the weather got better. There were many hotels to choose from and soon we located just the right place, our comfy refuge where we could relax for a few days before finding somewhere more long-term to stay. After our cold journey we wanted to treat ourselves. We ended up splashing out, spending two days worth of our budget on a single night. But we felt absolutely justified in doing so. There was no doubt, we deserved a bit of luxury. Our room was spotless and faultless. All seemed very new and was finished with quality materials. The place was perfect.

The hotel room was so comfortable that we didn't want to leave. The trouble was that we were getting hungry and the only food we had, had to be cooked. Having spent a small fortune on the accommodation, we decided to save on food and cook simple meals inside the hotel room. We had all we needed; pasta, a few vegetables and spices.

It wasn't the first time we'd used our petrol cooker indoors; we'd done it a few times before and it always worked just fine. Initially there's some dark smoke and a strong smell of burning petrol, but as the cooker warms up, it all disappears. Usually I cook on a windowsill, where ventilation is best; I just have to watch out not to burn the curtains.

To prepare the food, we divided our duties. My task was to get the cooker going, while Rebecca's was getting the ingredients ready. One by one, she began pulling things out of the kitchen bag; things that we needed for our meal. Then suddenly something exploded. The noise was loud and surprising enough to make me jump. When I turned around, the room looked like a scene from a horror movie, dripping with thick red liquid. It wasn't blood, though.

The explosion came from a small plastic tub, which Rebecca had just placed on the table. We used it to store tomato paste. Stirred by the movement, some strange reaction took place inside and as a result, the contents ended up all over the stylish five star hotel room. A clean-up operation began. We started with the walls. Luckily they were covered with quality wallpaper so the paste came off easily. There was nothing we could do about the bedding. It had to be machine washed. The ceiling was the hardest part to clean. I rubbed it ferociously with a wet cloth, but my efforts were making little difference. Barely noticeable was the best I could manage. It had to do. Cleaning the room took over an hour. By the time we'd finished, we'd lost our appetites and collapsed on the bed.

Later we tried to figure out what could have caused the explosion. The clue was in the packaging. Whilst in Greece, Rebecca's friend had sent us a small gift from the UK; a tub of marmite (yeast extract spread). Once we'd used it all up, we decided to reuse the tub, as it was light, durable and airtight. We washed and filled it with tomato paste from a glass jar. That was it; given the right conditions, the leftover yeast quickly multiplied inside. The tub was strong enough to allow the pressure to build up, but only to a certain point. Unfortunately, that point was reached in the hotel room. Unknowingly, we'd created a small explosive device, which exploded all over the first ever five star hotel we'd stayed in.

It was obvious that staying in hotels wasn't a good long-term strategy for us. Firstly, it was too expensive and secondly, we didn't want to make a habit of cooking in hotel rooms. It was just too risky. Then again, camping wasn't an option either. We needed to find a comfortable place where we could stay for longer, something relatively cheap, and with a kitchen.

Once again, CouchSurfing came to the rescue, but this time in a different way we were used to. We contacted a few people, asking if they would be interested in renting their spare room to us for a reasonable price. We got some responses and that's how we came into contact with Yilmaz.

Yilmaz liked the idea and was willing to negotiate. He was happy to gain some extra income and it worked for us, too. It was very unlikely we would find a similar room with access to a kitchen for a better price. Before even arriving, we committed ourselves to one month in his place, with the possibility of extending our stay for another month.

Our first impression was very positive. The apartment was in a quiet neighbourhood, with a fenced parking lot and 24h security, meaning that we didn't have to worry about leaving the motorcycle outside. Our room was nice too, exactly as in the pictures he'd sent us. There was a large kitchen with all utensils, and a sufficiently sized bathroom. The internet was fast and our double bed was pretty comfortable, too. We were happy.

Within a few hours of arriving, we realised that the apartment was pretty cold. There was no central heating in the building and our air conditioning unit was broken. The cold wasn't too bad, but it meant that we had to wear extra layers of clothing around the house, including hats and gloves. It was still a bargain. It had its kinks, but we liked the place.

As for Yilmaz, he was a mystery to us. Days after moving in, we found out that he'd given us his own bedroom and moved to the spare room, where he was sleeping on a mattress. He was a part-time piano teacher who detested his job: possibly because by nature he was quiet and withdrawn. It was only after some alcohol that he became animated and chatty. He was a kind soul, but somehow we could never truly connect. More than anything, he liked his personal space. He also liked drinking coffee, but while we made ours in the traditional Turkish way, he drank instant and insisted that it was the best type of coffee and that we must try it.

In our spare time, which we had heaps of, we explored the city. The centre was quite far, but busses were frequent and inexpensive. Occasionally we'd try some local dishes, but we mostly ate at home. For once we weren't limited by what we could cook on a camping stove. It was nice to take advantage of a full size kitchen. For our shopping we found a local bazaar and went there every couple of days. It was an enjoyable experience, even the mandatory haggling. One day I noticed that vendors gave me better prices when I was without Rebecca. By using a few Turkish words and looking like a Turk, I was blending in easily; whereas Rebecca, with her fair skin, freckles and bright red hair, had no chance of doing so, at least not in this part of the country. Interestingly, there is one area in northern Turkey, where her colouring is very common.

After a few weeks in Antalya, we began feeling restless. We'd fallen into a routine and needed to get out of the flat, even if only for a couple of days. After a quick bit of research, we decided to visit the Flaming Rocks of Chimaera. It wasn't a long drive, but it was an important one. This trip would determine whether the weather was good enough to continue our journey.

We left one Friday afternoon. Being back on the bike felt good. We slowly drove west, along the coast, enjoying every moment. A couple of hours later, not far from our destination, we came across two other bikers. It just wasn't the right season, so we hadn't seen anybody travelling on a motorcycle for months. It was exciting to finally meet other travellers, similar to us.

Barry and his father Neil were from Australia. They'd wanted to drive all the way to South Africa, but their journey was halted in Egypt, simply because they didn't have carnets de passage (CDPs). Back in Turkey, Barry and Neil were also finding themselves limited by the winter conditions. We had a lot in common and decided to spend the next few days together.

All of us were looking for accommodation, so I suggested driving to a nearby place with tree houses. Barry and Neil liked the idea and we headed there together. The place was almost empty. This was good because we could choose the best tree houses for a knock-down price. There were around ten to choose from, along with a few standard rooms on the ground. The owner almost laughed at us when he heard that we wanted to stay up a tree. He was convinced that it was way too cold. Probably feeling a bit sorry for the four of us, he offered a "normal" room for the same price. But that's not what we wanted; our minds were set on tree houses, whether it was a good idea, or not. After some initial resistance, we were finally allowed to choose our trees. As we chose beds, the owner went to get some extra blankets.

We quickly realised that calling this tree construction a "house" was a huge exaggeration. They were shacks, and badly made ones too. The walls had more holes than Swiss cheese, and the whole frame was wonky, so neither doors nor windows closed properly. It felt almost like sleeping outside. And the owner was right, it was freezing at night. To stay warm, Rebecca and I gathered all the blankets we had, connected our sleeping bags and curled up together in one of the single bunk beds. If nothing else, it was romantic. For the first time in our lives, we were sleeping in a tree house, and we loved it.

What's more, staying there was cheap. And I mean dirt cheap. For just a couple of pounds a night, we had our own tree shack (sorry, house) and could help ourselves to a complimentary buffet breakfast and lunch. Anywhere else, we'd have paid more for food alone. It was even cheaper than staying at Yilmaz's place.

Those days away from Antalya were exactly what we needed. It connected us with other people and with our own goals. It showed us that the weather had improved and indeed, we'd very soon be able to continue with our journey.

Bitter-sweet

By January we'd became totally bored with Antalya. We were eager to hit the road, but having paid for our room one month in advance, we didn't want to leave before we'd used up that time. Luckily, there was little time left. So we waited it out. By the time our rent had finished, the weather had improved significantly. It was definitely time to make a move. Our next destination was Georgia.

We knew that getting there wasn't going to be easy. The weather had got better, but the winter was still hanging around in many parts of Turkey. To prepare ourselves for the journey, we bought some extra layers from a second hand shop and equipped the motorcycle with hand warmers for me; an idea I copied from Turkish bikers. Truth be told, with those elbow-long sleeves attached, the motorcycle looked more suitable for a takeaway delivery service than for an intercontinental motorcycle adventure. I had to swallow my pride. It was comfort and safety that mattered, not looks.

Ready for our coast to coast journey, we packed the motorcycle and left Antalya for good. We planned to go east, along the coast, until ready to turn north and cut right through the heart of Turkey, through parts that were still wintery.

First on our route was Gaziantep, known as the Turkish capital of Baklava. It was just getting dark when we entered the city. As a general rule, we try not to drive after sunset, but on this occasion we had little choice; we just couldn't find a suitable hotel and circled around the city for ages. Everything was either way too expensive or just too dingy. There was nothing in between. Even the most rundown smelly rooms came with an expensive price tag.

After a long and tiring search, we found something that was just about acceptable for one night. Even though it was already late, we didn't want to leave the next day without trying some famous Gaziantep baklava. Minutes after checking in, we were out the door. Shops selling baklava were literally everywhere. Inside were hundreds, maybe even thousands of varieties. The choice seemed endless. We gave ourselves permission to go wild and eat as much as we could.

Gaziantep is famous for pistachio baklava, which, after the first taste, we understood was in a completely different league to cheaper varieties. It's said that Gaziantep is the home of the best baklava in the world. After having tried some, we think it may very well be true.

We decided to pace ourselves but to try as many different kinds of baklava as possible. Strolling from one shop to another, we searched for the most visually appealing types. The only problem was that they all looked delicious. Once we'd made our minds up, we asked in broken Turkish for "Only two pieces, please" and pointed at the ones we wanted. In each shop we visited, the person behind the counter seemed to find this request most confusing. The reason for that wasn't our bad Turkish (although it was indeed terrible and raised a few brows), but the unusual nature of our request. For them it was unheard of to ask for only two pieces of baklava. But that was all we wanted before moving on to another shop. On a few occasions we were given our two pieces for free. It was a kind gesture we were more than happy to accept.

In one of the shops, I pulled the money out of my wallet and had it ready to pay, only to be told to put it away; once again the baklava was a gift. We took the sweets, gave our thanks and left. As we were walking away, peacefully enjoying our delicacies, we heard somebody calling us from behind. I turned around, surprised, and saw it was the guy who'd just served us. He handed me a large bill that I had dropped a minute earlier in his shop.

I have to admit that I wasn't too keen on the city when we first arrived, but after receiving all that kindness, sweetness and honesty, how could I not like Gaziantep. Satisfied with our visit and all sugared out, the next morning we were ready to move on. Gaziantep was as far east as we needed to come. It was finally time to start heading north.

Next we drove to Malatya. To get there, we had to pass through some mountain ranges. The route was beautiful; one of the most scenic routes we'd ever seen. But it was also one of the most challenging ones. The temperature was around zero degrees centigrade and in many places the outer parts of the road were covered in ice. It was hard to see the frozen patches, until we were right up close. To make it even more challenging, occasionally there were large chunks of rocks scattered on the road. And as if that wasn't enough, in some places oil spills were almost impossible to avoid, thanks to the ever-present HGV lorries that used the roads. Altogether, it was every motorcyclist's nightmare! We were pretty well prepared to face the cold, but once again I found myself outside my comfort zone when it came to driving. But there was no way back, we had to keep moving forward, even if only at the most cautious pace.

The route wasn't all bad, though. The landscape was stunning and was changing constantly. Mineral rich soil would throw a range of colours at us. When mountains turned red, it almost felt as if we were driving on Mars. At other times the whole area turned blue or green, or suddenly we'd find ourselves in a land of snow, where hills and mountain peaks were covered in white powder.

We arrived at our destination in the late afternoon, many hours later than planned, but still in one piece (well, two pieces). We could finally relax and reflect on the journey, which had been a strange blend of beauty and danger. The challenge was over and there was a warm feeling of achievement and relief within us. We were worn out and just wanted a comfortable bed to rest in, so we booked ourselves into the first hotel we saw. It was basic and overpriced, but we had no energy left in us to keep going. It had to do.

After checking in, Rebecca stayed in the room while I went to the motorcycle to bring our things. I returned a few minutes later and found my wife bent in half on the floor. She was crying in agony. I had no idea what the hell had happened. I tried to ask, but she was in so much pain that she couldn't talk. I was scared and didn't know what to do. Next to Rebecca, also on the floor, was a large heavy wooden window frame. It looked like it had fallen on her shoulder. I ran to the reception for some ice. A cold compress helped with relieving some pain and after a short while Rebecca was able to speak. She explained that she'd tried to open the window, which was located high above her head, and as she touched it, the frame fell on her shoulder, missing her head by inches. The impact left her in excruciating pain.

It was possible that her arm was broken. There was some mobility so we decided not to drive to the hospital, but instead to wait and see how she felt a bit later.

As for the hotel staff, soon after the accident we were given another room, but not a single word of apology. They didn't seem to care at all. I was livid. Because of the pain, Rebecca couldn't sleep that night. We really wanted to leave the next morning, but her arm was swollen and painful; painful enough that putting her motorcycle jacket on was too much to bear. There was no other choice; we had to stay at least another day in this damned hotel.

In the morning, I went to the reception to explain our situation and confirm that we needed to stay another day. Still, there was no remorse, even though the accident was basically their fault. When I said that I didn't want to pay the full price for our second night, the owner got defensive and angry with me. Imagine. To my mind, I shouldn't have had to pay anything. But in this place I had to fight for a discount. It was an outcry. In the end I paid half. Fortunately the pain had decreased after the second night, at least enough for Rebecca to get her jacket on. We left the next day and continued going north, taking the shortest route to Georgia. The border was getting close and we felt excited about it.

Not long before the crossing, we pulled over for a short rest in a tea house. It was going to be our last Turkish tea. The owner welcomed us with smiles and quickly brought drinks to the table. He was curious about our journey and wanted to know where we'd been, and whether we liked Turkey. We still felt bitter about the window incident, but kept it to ourselves. Talking about all the nice places we'd visited on our way helped us lighten up and forget about the falling window frame. Later when we'd finished our drinks and asked to pay, he showed that it was a gift from the heart. This small gesture was exactly what we needed; a reminder that the world is full of kind and caring people, quite a few of whom we met on our travels in Turkey. His generosity was a precious gift, far beyond the price of two cups of tea.

The wild west

It was bucketing down when we neared the Turkish-Georgian border. There was a long line of waiting vehicles, but we just drove straight passed them and swiftly arrived at the checkpoint. I was worried that on the Turkish side there may be some records of our unpaid highway bills, but none of the officers mentioned anything. They just stamped our passports and let us through. We left Turkey and entered no man's land, one step closer to Georgia. Ahead of us was the final check point.

Usually border control personnel are not the friendliest bunch of people, but Georgians were different. To our surprise, they were joking and laughing, and even gave us a short language lesson. As expected, they didn't ask for insurance documents, nor even for a driving license, there was no customs paperwork to be filled in, or checking of the luggage. It was easy and quite enjoyable; a pretty good start.

It was still raining when we entered the country. Road conditions and the way people drove immediately worsened. We already knew that Georgia was notorious for road accidents and our worries were immediately confirmed; they were terrible drivers. Also, in Georgia there's no obligatory vehicle inspection, so any vehicle that moves is allowed on the road. It seemed to mean that all the junk from other countries ended up in Georgia. We'd entered the wild west (or the wild east); the land without rules where anything goes.

It didn't take long before we felt in danger. Already within the first hour, I had to swerve out of the way to avoid a head-on collision. Not once, but a few times. Cars were overtaking regardless of vehicles coming from the opposite direction. They usually somehow made enough space for each other. The idea of keeping a safe distance just didn't exist here. It was bedlam. But that was their way of driving and I had to adjust; the quicker the better. As for motorcycles, they might as well be invisible. The main rule of the road was simple; the biggest vehicle wins. It didn't help that ours seemed to be the only motorcycle on the road.

In my attempt to blend in and stay safe, first I tried driving assertively. I positioned the bike firmly in the middle of the lane and tried my best not to be bullied. But soon enough someone would start tailing me, only a few inches behind the bike. Eventually they'd overtake in the most impossible of situations, endangering themselves and us in the process. And this scenario kept repeating itself. You may think that I drove too slowly, but no. The thing is that in Georgia there are three speed categories; slow, very fast and freaking stupidly fast. I went with very fast, together with the majority of drivers. Still, it was way beyond the speed limit. The next category, slow, is reserved only for heavy armoured vehicles, like tractors and other tank-like machines. Stupidly fast drivers are just lunatics, people (most often men) without imagination or the will to live. Surprisingly they seemed pretty common.

So once I knew that assertive wasn't my best strategy, I switched to a more defensive style; driving on the side of the road. But that was like an open invitation for others to push forward and eventually force me further to the side.

There wasn't one best way for every situation. I had to continuously adjust, depending on what was happening around me. Sometimes that meant overtaking and speeding, sometimes hiding on the side and letting others pass. Anything that made us feel even a tiny bit safer was thrown into the mix of our survival strategies. For example, on a relatively empty road, following a fast car was a good idea. This way I was protected from a head-on collision, and if we drove fast enough, no one else would push in from behind. I just had to find a driver worth following, somebody in the top of the very fast category, but still reasonable enough not to qualify for the freaking stupidly fast category.

Needless to say, driving in Georgia was very stressful, but luckily we didn't have to go far the first day. Batumi, our next destination, was only thirty miles away from the Turkish border. By the time we reached the city we were drenched and exhausted. To make matters worse, we got lost and circled for another hour before finding our bearings.

It was supposed to be a quick easy drive that day, but turned out to be the exact opposite. It was already dark by the time we arrived at the gates of our hostel. We were tired, cold and hungry. We rang the bell and patiently waited for somebody to come and open the gate, but nobody came. We tried again and waited even longer, but still there were no signs of life. After about twenty minutes we were ready to leave, when suddenly an old man came out of the hostel. He slowly came over and began talking, in Russian. We couldn't understand each other, but somehow made do with a handful of words and plenty of gestures. After a lot of effort from both sides, he put us in one of the rooms. This long day was finally over. We dropped on our bed and instantly fell asleep.

God's own land

The hostel was great. It was just outside the city, located on a hillside, amongst orange and kiwi groves. The area was good for walking and relaxing, two things which we highly value.

We were given a comfortable en-suite room, with access to the shared kitchen. The bike was safely stored just outside our window. There were plenty of shops nearby, one of which was selling delicious cheap baked Georgian snacks. We soon almost became addicted to them. Also, if we ever wanted, the grandfather that checked us in was selling homemade wine and moonshine for a very reasonable price.

We quickly realised that Georgia is very unique. The story explaining the genesis of the country reflects it, both in terms of the culture and the beauty of their land. So the story goes; when God was dividing the Earth, people lined up to be given their share. All except Georgians, who were so engaged in drinking wine, eating tasty food, singing and dancing that they turned up late. By the time they arrived, the entire Earth had already been divided, nations had been created and there was nothing left for them. When God asked to what they had been drinking, Georgians cheerfully answered "To you, Lord, to us and to peace". Touched by their spirit, God revealed that there was still a small plot of land which belonged to God himself, but he said the Georgians could have it. That land was incomparable in its beauty and all people would admire and cherish it forever. It is now known as Georgia. There is something that rings true about this story; the country is truly outstanding and its people are just like the story portrays them, hedonistic and untamed.

Georgia has what we value the most when travelling; nature and people, both fascinating and worthy of getting to know much better. Here, we felt welcomed and at home. Besides, it was very easy to be a tourist in Georgia. To encourage more visitors, almost every nationality was allowed to stay in the country for up to a year visa-free.

There was one more reason why we were glad to have come to Georgia; it was the ease of flying out and leaving the motorcycle behind. Here nobody cared that we had temporarily imported a vehicle. For us that was actually a big deal. It meant no fuss if we wanted to fly back to Europe. In Turkey, for example, I read that leaving a vehicle not only involves going through an ambiguous and overcomplicated process at the customs office, but is also very costly. In Georgia it was free and simple (i.e. unregulated) and that suited us perfectly.

Our good friends back home had invited us to their wedding and it was a day we couldn't miss. Being in Georgia, we could fly back easily leaving the bike ready to later continue our adventure. Soon after our arrival we booked flights knowing we could relax about the motorcycle being safe behind the hostel gate. Before our "holiday", we had a few more days left to explore Batumi.

Comrades

One afternoon, a couple of days before our flight, we went out exploring the hills near our hostel. Long into our walk, we came across a traditional wooden house with a Georgian family passing time outside. Everyone curiously looked at us, so we greeted them in the local language. The father came over and started talking to us in Russian. We only knew a few basic phrases, but it was enough to answer his questions. After telling him where we were from, he warmed up even more and asked us to be his guests. Within just a few minutes, the family had brought out a small table, chairs, a couple of bottles of alcohol and some sweets to share with us.

Even before we sat down, he'd already filled our glasses with wine and proudly announced that it was homemade. So we raised a toast and drank. The wine wasn't anything like we'd tried before; it wasn't good, but it wasn't bad either, it was just different. Shortly after, he offered us something stronger. It wasn't vodka but infamous Georgian chacha, also homemade. Chacha is for serious drinking as it can reach even 65% in strength. I'd never tried it before and thought that it was as good a time as ever to go for it. Rebecca wisely declined.

The shot was the size of a small teacup. I gathered my courage and gulped it down in one. This stuff was like rocket fuel; my eyes popped and throat started burning. In the heat of the Georgian sun, I felt almost instantly drunk. Wine was definitely a safer option if I were to last a little bit longer. The father was laughing. He could tell I wasn't a drinker. After a couple more drinks, our host brought a large atlas in Russian and asked us to show him our cities. He knew both Poland and Wales very well; Poland because he'd been stationed there as a young soviet soldier, and Wales because of Swansea City football club. He also brought an English-Russian dictionary which helped our communication a lot, beside more chacha.

It was from him that we first learned about the Georgian sentiment toward Polish people. There are a few reasons for it. One is pretty simple; it's just because Georgians are familiar with Poland, often more than with other European countries. There are many Georgian people who either study or work in Poland. Also, during communism, a lot of young men were sent there as soldiers. But, most probably, the main reason for this national fondness of Poles is that during the Russo-Georgian war in 2008, the Polish president Lech Kaczynski backed Georgia against Russia. He even arrived in Tbilisi with other politicians to show his support, thereby risking his own life. This meant a lot to Georgians. Later Kaczynski was named a National Hero of Georgia for "showing heroism in defending Georgia's interests". Many Georgians strongly believe that Kaczynski died in the plane crash two years later as a direct consequence of his stance against Russia. After the accident, the Georgian president, Saakashvili, said that "there is something incredibly evil" about the tragic death of the Polish President, insinuating that it was Russia's doing.

Never ending

It was early February when we parted with our motorcycle, leaving it locked up behind the gates of our Batumi hostel. We knew it would be safe there during our absence. The bus journey to the airport took just two hours and as expected, the bus driver was pretty reckless, doing all sorts of crazy things to get us there as fast as he could. The rollercoaster driving style was accompanied by banging Russian disco music in the background and a dense plume of cigarette smoke. The driver made it safely to the airport, which he celebrated with another cigarette, but this time slowly savouring each puff.

I was worried about going through customs. Even though I'd spoken with a few other bikers who'd left their motorcycles behind while leaving the country for a spell, I still thought that the customs officials may stop and question me about my bike. I even made up some unreal story in my mind, hoping it would get me out of trouble if necessary. Luckily, they knew nothing about the motorcycle and let me through without the slightest problem.

When back in Europe, we first stayed with my side of the family in Poland. It was a short two-day stopover before flying further, to the UK. I used that time in Poland to do some essential shopping; I bought a set of sprockets and a new chain.

Then we flew to the UK, where we spent another few days. Our holiday, though short, was a needed break from the motorcycle. We were spoiled by our families and enjoyed catching up with friends. On our way back over to Georgia, we stayed one more night in Poland. I packed my shopping and the next morning my dad drove us to the airport. We said our goodbyes at the car and let him slowly return home.

As we were going through security, my hand-luggage got picked out for further searching. The scanner picked up the rear sprocket that I'd recently bought. It wasn't allowed on the plane. I'd made a mistake; I never thought of a sprocket as being a potential weapon, not even for a second. I was asked to remove it from my luggage and to hand it over to be binned. My dad was long gone so there was nobody to give it to. I guessed that checking-in this piece of metal would probably cost more than it was worth. On the other hand, binning it seemed like a waste of money. Either way, I had to make a quick decision. Thinking that I had no other choice, I reluctantly placed it in the bin. It wasn't an easy decision, but I was glad that the other sprocket and the chain were still inside my luggage. The front sprocket was much more important to me, so I accepted the loss.

I was ready to move on when the officer requested to put my luggage through the scanner once again. I was busted. This time they picked up the front sprocket. For a moment I tried to argue that it was so small that it could just as well be a piece of jewellery or a belt buckle, but it didn't work. If anything, it made the officer even angrier. He definitely didn't share my logic. This time the loss was harder to swallow. There was no way I could throw away both my sprockets. Things like this were irreplaceable in Georgia. I needed that damn sprocket and my only option was to check it in.

Suddenly the light bulb in my brain came on. If I was going to pay to check one of them in, I might as well check in the two and the chain. I had to do it, I had to ask the officer to open the bin. I was a nuisance, I know, but I had a plan. I realised that I didn't have to lose any money. My request didn't go down well. They didn't even know where the key was. I was holding up the queue and making a bit of a scene in the process. I was a polite persistent pest, though. They were beyond impatient, but they also wanted me gone. After a few minutes one of the officers agreed to help me and went looking for the key. He opened the bin and I got my sprocket back. I was back to square one, but at least I had a sense of what needed to be done.

Before heading off I asked about my new motorcycle chain, which still lied undiscovered in my luggage. To my utter surprise they said that I could take that on board; no problem. After all the fuss about my sprockets, I couldn't believe it.

With both sprockets in hand, I ran to the check-in desk, hoping that it was open. There were still a few people forming a small line. I joined them. As I waited, another idea popped into my head; why not ask someone else to take them for me. These sprockets were pretty light and compact so it wouldn't be much trouble to add them to check-in luggage. In front of me was a young couple with a child, about to hand over their luggage. I approached them and pretty much begged them to take my sprockets. They agreed without hesitation. It seemed I had more luck than common sense that day. I got my sprockets back a few hours later in Georgia. I kept them safely in my hands when we left the airport. We quickly boarded the bus and patiently waited for the other passengers to come and fill all the seats, but there weren't enough people going to Batumi. After a while, we were moved to another, much smaller bus and off we went.

Somehow all bus journeys in Georgia start with an obligatory stop at a petrol station. We barely drove for ten minutes before pulling over. Most other passengers got out, either for a cigarette or to buy something for the road. We stayed put. Suddenly I realised that one of my sprockets was missing. It was in my hand when we got on the first bus so I must have left it there. Once again, I'd lost it. And once again, I had to get it back. After all that had happened in the airport back in Poland, I wasn't going to give up easily at the last hurdle. The whole situation was a shambles. I ran to the driver and threw my desperate pleas at him. My Russian was beyond limited, but I was trying my best. I must have used every single word in my vocabulary because after a few minutes of pestering him, I actually managed to persuade the guy to drive back. He agreed, reluctantly. For him time was money and my mindlessness would cost him at least an extra half an hour. Other passengers also seemed a bit annoyed about the delay.

Ten minutes later we were back at the airport, but it was too late. The bus and my sprocket had departed a few minutes earlier. If there was ever a time to give up, that was it. Nobody would have blamed me for not putting up a fight. Before losing my final shreds of hope, I dashed to the customer service desk, just to ask one last time. And it was lucky I did; these guys were excellent. They reached for the phone right away and after a couple of minutes joyfully exclaimed that I could have it back. Somebody was actually sent to fetch it for me. Absolutely unbelievable! I was assured that I'd have my sprocket back within a few minutes.

Twenty minutes later and we were still waiting. Tension was running high. By then we were delayed by about an hour. Everybody was peeved and impatient. I could only offer my apologies and ask for a few minutes more. Finally the sprocket arrived. This time I wasn't going to take my eyes of it.

Open doors

We returned to Batumi. The plan was to stay for a few months, at least while the weather was still unpredictable. The tropical climate in Batumi suited us well. As much as we liked our hostel, we knew we could get a better deal for our money someplace else. While over in the UK, Rebecca had done some research and found an apartment for rent on AirBnB. She contacted the owner and negotiated a good deal for us. We moved in within days of getting back in the city.

We liked our new place. It was old fashioned, "babushka style" as we called it. It was fully furnished, almost as if some Georgian granny still lived there. We instantly grew fond of this place. Conveniently, our new home was located pretty much right in the city centre. We just didn't know what to do with all the space. The place was enormous for our modest needs. So after some thinking, we decided to use all the extra space to increase our good karma; it was time to repay our CouchSurfing debt and to give back to the hosting community. We opened up to accommodating other travellers.

There was another reason for inviting strangers to our home; we felt the need to connect with other people. Travelling on a motorcycle can often feel lonely. Winter was that time for us. And from our experience, using CouchSurfing was a great opportunity to meet interesting people.

Requests to host came in thick and fast; we were receiving more than we could accommodate. Our preference was to host couples, as we'd instantly have things in common, but we didn't make it a rule. We stayed open to all requests, from people from all walks of life.

We had guests almost every day. But with so many people visiting us, it quickly became costly. Initially we shared everything, expecting nothing in return. Soon we realised that we couldn't go on like this; our budget was already strained by the rent, so we made it clear on our profile that we were happy to provide a place to stay, our company and a delicious breakfast, but in return we'd expected guests to cook a shared meal per day and to help with the cleaning. We thought it was a fair deal and requests continued coming as before.

Two of our most memorable guests were Rafal and Gosia, from Poland. They were hitchhiking their way to Australia. Having planned to go through Iran, they needed visas, and Batumi was one of the places to get them. The application process took a while, and they ended up staying with us for over a week. That meant we got to know each other pretty well, and soon became friends.

One day, while exploring Batumi, we noticed dolphins, happily swimming near the shore, not further than hundred feet away. The idea of swimming towards them was born, probably as a joke, but soon the thought of actually reaching them, right in their natural habitat, became a serious consideration. One problem was that it was a cold day, not more than ten degrees centigrade. The sea was even colder.

The dolphins were close enough to feel them within our reach. I was definitely tempted. Gosia was hesitant at first. Rebecca and Rafal were happy to look from a safe distance. We all knew it would be a bone-chilling challenge, but I believed we could do it. Soon Gosia too was willing to try. It was a crazy idea, but once we'd both set our minds to it, we were unstoppable.

Believing that preparation was key to success, we rushed back home to change into our swimsuits and to grab some blankets. Rebecca made hot tea to take back to the shore with us. We were so excited that we almost sprinted back to the beach. It was a good way to prepare, as with the run our bodies warmed up significantly. Once we got back to the beach, Gosia and I quickly got ready. The objective was simple; get in the water, swim there and back as quickly as possible before we froze.

Without wasting any time, we walked into the sea. The initial few seconds felt good; the water didn't seem too cold. Even more than before, I felt encouraged to continue and submerged my whole body. Suddenly the cold hit me; I lost my breath and my legs felt as if they were on fire. It hadn't even been a minute. Gosia and I looked at each other; we were experiencing exactly the same sensations. Without a single word, we both knew that staying wasn't an option and got out immediately.

A couple of days after Gosia and Rafal left, we received new guests, this time from Iran. Araf and Soude had never before been abroad but had very well defined expectations. They wanted to dance in public, drink alcohol and eat pork; all three being forbidden in their home country. The request seemed easy enough and we tried our best to accommodate it, starting with a bottle of Georgian wine.

Araf was an amateur filmmaker and knew everything about Iranian cinematography. He inspired me to start making short videos and showed me how to use editing software. Soude, on the other hand, recommended some excellent movies from Iran.

They were the first people from Iran we'd ever met. We'd had no real expectations about meeting Araf and Soude, but were surprised to see that despite coming from such a different culture to ours, they were actually so much alike us, with similar interests, dreams, relationship troubles, tastes in music, films and food. Yet there was one huge difference between us, we had the freedom that they could only dream of. We could travel the world, freely express our ideas and follow the lifestyle of our choice. For Araf and Soude it was very different. They told us about people their age being arrested and thrown into prison for even the smallest of offences against the social and political order. We were moved to hear that despite being in love, their marriage was more a necessity than a choice. We could sense their pain and helplessness when talking about Iran. In spite of it all, they deeply loved their country and had hope for a better future. We'd have liked to visit them in Tehran, but Rebecca's visa application was rejected.

Not long after Araf and Soude left, Jake came, another one of our most memorable guests. He was from Australia, but was temporarily living and working in Tbilisi, the capital of Georgia. He was staying for free in a hostel in exchange for his work; something similar to what we did on the farm in Greece. Jake came across as a free spirit and his looks reflected it. He didn't seem to care about fashion, quite the opposite; his clothes were shabby and worn, and his long ginger beard was wild and ragged. There was nothing hipster about Jake. If anything, he looked like a hobo, and in many ways (just like Rebecca and I) he was exactly that. Jake had been on the road for years, wandering from place to place, mostly hitchhiking, occasionally CouchSurfing, often doing odd jobs in exchange for food and accommodation. Yet Jake was the kind of guy you instantly want to become friends with. He was easygoing, open-minded, curious about the world and always saw the best in people and places. It was a pleasure to spend a few days in his company.

We also had guests from other countries, such as Ukraine, India, America, France, Germany, Turkey and many more. Our apartment became one of the most international places in Batumi. We enjoyed building a small community of travellers around us. It was our goal to connect with other people and having an apartment in Batumi gave us exactly that opportunity, and we were grateful for it.

The kitschy city

Some people love Batumi, some really dislike it. That's just the way it is. Maybe it's a matter of expectations, maybe of personal taste. It's hard to say. For us Batumi was a place of rest and a base to explore the region.

The city itself felt spacious and calm, and was almost deserted during our stay. Maybe in the peak of tourist season it's different, overcrowded and confined, but that wasn't the Batumi we got to know and experienced. It is a strange city, though. Millions of dollars have been invested to raise its appeal as a seaside resort, resulting in the construction of many architectural monstrosities and tasteless "attractions". Ever-present, brighter-than-day colourful neon lights are just the icing on the cake. Visitors are left confused, not knowing whether they should admire the effort or laugh in disbelieve. Some people go as far as to say that Batumi is not "real Georgia", but it's as real as it can get. It's a sad reflection of the government and its inability to invest wisely, and a reminder of socio-economic divisions, increasingly more visible in modern Georgia.

In addition to its tasteless image, Batumi has built a reputation of being a city of sin; a place where gambling and drinking are the allure for many – alcohol is even said to flow from a public fountain in season as if it were water. Indeed, for some it's a promised land, especially for Turks where such temptations are often out of reach in their own country.

Despite its kitschy facade, we soon realised that Batumi is more than meets the eye. It isn't the grotesque architecture or cheap thrills, but local people that are at the heart of the city. Everywhere we looked it was evident that Batumi is a sociable place. People gather everywhere they can; by ponds, near fountains, in the main park, along the promenade, in the port, central square, cafés, restaurants, and in many other places.

One such place was almost right outside of our apartment. Every day, without exception, there was at least one small group of people, especially guys, gathered around a car. It looked like a mini party, with sweets, sometimes fruit and other snacks, and of course plenty of alcohol spread out across the car bonnet. It seemed strange, even for Georgia. One day we decided to find out what it was all about. We went and asked. The answer was simple; there was a maternity hospital opposite our apartment. They were celebrating a newborn baby. The answer came with an invitation to join and wet the baby's head. We couldn't say no. They were too friendly, and anyway, we wouldn't want to have jinxed the baby by refusing to drink to its health. The second time we were asked to join in, we were spotted hanging laundry on our balcony. I don't know, maybe in Georgia it's a good omen having a foreigner raising a toast for a newborn; we were in demand. It was fun to be included, but only the first few times. After a while we knew better to avoid any eye contact, unless of course we wanted to get merry.

Some of our favourite spaces in Batumi were those allocated to playing games. These were always busy, especially with older man. Chess was most popular and was taken very seriously. Spectators often gathered to watch. We too, liked watching.

Living in Batumi, soon we developed habits, small ways to enjoy ourselves. Each morning we walked to our favourite patisserie. It almost became our daily ritual. There, for a very decent price, we treated ourselves to a tasty cup of coffee and at least one cake to go with it. The place was always busy with young Georgians hanging out with friends. We also had a favourite restaurant, a place that couldn't be matched, not for price, not for taste. It was a culinary treasure that was little known to tourists but overflowing with locals. When we arrived there the first time, we disliked it. Each party had its own cubicle and could enjoy the privacy of their enclosure. For us, at first, it felt isolating and a bit claustrophobic. It took away the chance to do one of our favourite things while travelling - people watching. Shortly it became clear that being in a cubicle had one massive advantage; it protected us from the dense cloud of cigarette smoke, so common in Georgian bars and restaurants. We liked this place so much that we took most of our Couch Surfing guests there.

Another place that we considered a must-see was the main bazaar. Going there became one of our favourite pastimes. It was situated just on the outskirts of Batumi. It was easy to get there; either on foot or by bus. The area seemed like a completely different city; less glamorous, busier, more rural and down to earth, yet at the same time more fun. The way things are in Georgia, we could always count on buying things fresher and cheaper in the bazaar than in a supermarket. We made it our goal to only shop there, not only because it was cheaper, but also because buying produce directly from locals was good fun and felt much better than giving to supermarket chains. There would almost always be somebody offering us free food samples. The most common things to try were pickles, cheeses, or homemade alcohol; especially alcohol, and it was given in generous quantities. A few times I left the bazaar pretty tipsy after tasting too much chacha.

The snow is melting

For almost two months, our guests had been sharing their adventure stories with us and now, we too, wanted to start collecting more of our own stories from the road. The spring was our gateway.

The rent on our apartment was coming to an end, so it was time to consider our options and decide what we wanted to do next. The whole of Georgia was waiting to be explored. First though, we had some unfinished business with Turkey. We realised that there was so much more that we hadn't seen because of winter. We needed to go back. But before returning to Turkey, we decided to do at least a couple of weekend motorcycle trips in Georgia, kind of as a warm-up run.

Our first trip was pretty unorganised. We just wanted to get out there. The day before our departure, we simply looked at the map and chose our route. It wasn't even a proper road. But maybe that's exactly what attracted us to it. Also we noticed that if we followed it all the way, we would arrive in Vardzia, the cave city, one of the better known tourist attractions in Georgia. We were sold. There was only one small concern, the route cut right through a high mountain pass. Having in mind that it was still winter and that encountering some snow was pretty likely, I looked on the internet for any accounts of people driving through the pass. There was a video of some guys doing it in their 4x4. I decided that if they could do it in a car, I certainly could on my motorcycle.

We left on a Friday afternoon. It was a nice sunny day, perfect for biking. As we continued on our route, the mountains were slowly getting higher, forests denser, villages prettier and people more surprised to see us. The only thing gradually disappearing was the road surface. A few hours into our trip, tarmac became just a memory. We could tell that not many tourists made it that far from the look on people's faces. As we were getting closer to the mountain pass, the villagers began to look at as with concern. Some were showing "no go" by crossing their hands, others were telling us to go back. We continued regardless, curious to see how far we could get. Soon enough we realised that it was a dead end; the road suddenly turned into a snow covered mountain. That was it. We didn't make it to our destination, but where we ended up was really nice, great for camping. High in the mountains, the view was beautiful. There was even a small wooden shelter by the side of the road with just enough space for a tent, our tent. With not a single soul around, we expected a peaceful stay.

We'd just finished pitching our tent and were about to start cooking when a minibus full of locals showed up. It stopped right outside our shelter. A large group of people poured out through the door and came straight to us. For them, we were the "tourist attraction". Our visitors turned out to be a family from a nearby village. They seemed very friendly, and very curious. Soon enough, someone pulled out a bottle of chacha. I'd finished my driving for the day and was happy to share the drink. They only had one glass, so the bottle travelled from person to person. One of the guys went back to the minibus to turn the music on. It was traditional Georgian dance music, full volume. Suddenly we had a little party going, with the whole family dancing in a large circle. It was surreal.

It lasted for about an hour, before someone decided that it was time to move the party back to the house. We were also invited. If it wasn't for the surrounding nature, we would have agreed to head back with them, but we preferred a peaceful night with our mountain view. We kindly declined the offer. None of the family could understand why we'd choose to stay in a tent, not in a comfortable house. After insisting for another twenty minutes, they finally let us be and left. Though just before leaving they warned us about the wolves.

The next day we woke up to a magnificent sunrise. The air was still cold when we first left our tent. We were a bit disappointed, though, that not even one wolf had showed up at night to say hello.

For breakfast we had a bowl of porridge with bananas and raisins. It was tasty, and quickly warmed us up. There was no hurry to do anything, so we just sat on the grass and enjoyed the view. Far in the distance we spotted a tiny figure slowly walking in our direction. Half an hour later we could see it was an old man. He was carrying large plastic bottles in his hands. Another half an hour later, he'd finally made it to our shelter. We exchanged greetings and he continued past, up the mountain and through the snow. We were intrigued to know where he was going with those bottles. The next village was at least ten miles away, on the other side of the mountain pass. We didn't believe he was going there. I decided to find out. I grabbed my own plastic bottle and ran after him. After catching up, I asked in Russian "can I come?" which he approved with a smile. Together, we walked up the mountain for another ten minutes. The view was getting better with each step. Suddenly the old man became excited; we'd arrived.

There wasn't much there, except a sheet of metal with a few heavy stones on top. Underneath was a well. He uncovered it and then proudly poured me a cup of water. It was mineral water, very distinct and tasty. The old man tried to explain the health benefits, but I couldn't really understand. Whatever it was, it must have been worth his time and energy. Minutes later our bottles were full and we headed back down. The man had a long walk ahead of him and now he was heavily loaded. Before we even had time to thank him, he was gone. Soon after, we also headed off, slowly making our way back to Batumi.

Celebrating Easter

Exactly one week after our trip to the mountain pass, came Easter. The weather was still holding up, so we left the apartment once again. On this occasion we were better organised; we did proper research and found a good hiking destination near the town of Borjomi. We decided to use one of the main roads to get there; this time we wouldn't get lost or be distracted by some unexpected adventures. Our friends from Poland had come over to visit and were joining us. We planned to hit a trail together.

We arrived in Borjomi on a Friday afternoon. The town itself was not very special, but it's surrounded by mountains and over the years has become a gateway to the nearby national park. Our friends had already found a guesthouse by the time we met them. For us, the plan was to rough it. Our apartment in Batumi was left empty and we didn't want to pay double for accommodation. We decided to stay in our tent; just needed to find a relatively safe place to pitch it. But finding the right place proved more difficult than usual. There weren't any isolated sites, the kind of sites that we like most. We had no other option but to consider pitching it in somebody's garden. We drove around for a long time before we spotted something with potential. The place we found wasn't perfect, but at least the land was fenced and large enough to hide in a corner. We stopped by the gate. The land was to our right. To our left was a large house. They both seemed to be owned by the same people. As we stood there thinking whether we should try to ask somebody for permission to camp there, a woman came out of the house and approached us. She wanted to know if we needed any help. We tried explaining that we were looking for somewhere to pitch our tent, but she just called her husband and told us to talk to him. When the husband came, we repeated our request and got a positive response straight away. Our tent was up in no time The first night was very comfortable. We felt safe there and slept like logs. In the morning we decided that we could just leave our tent as it was and go off trekking for the day. It was out of sight and the woman who'd come out to greet us the previous day was pottering around. There wasn't much inside, but the tent itself and our sleeping bags were pretty precious to us. Still, it felt relatively comfortable leaving them behind, under a watchful eye. So that's what we did.

It was a long day in the mountains. The trails were very enjoyable but left us tired. By the time we got back to our tent, it was already dark. As expected, everything was as we'd left it. We were exhausted and eager to have some rest. A few minutes later we turned the lights off and hit the pillow. We were almost asleep when we heard footsteps. Somebody came right outside our tent. I immediately got up, unzipped the door and went outside. There was a man standing in front of me. It took me a moment to recognise that it was the guy on whose land we were camped. He must have waited for us to get back, with the intention of inviting us to his house.

That evening everyone was celebrating Easter in Georgia and his family was no exception. We didn't want to intrude, but opportunities like this happen rarely. Sleeping could wait; we had a party to attend. Excited, we quickly got dressed and went inside the house.

We were led to a dining room and introduced to the whole family, altogether around twenty people. The men were sitting around the dining table, drinking, while the women were taking care of the food. Kids were somewhere in between, running around the house and playing. As we sat, more food and drinks began to appear. The family had already eaten but wanted us to try everything. The amount of food was staggering. There were something like ten different cakes alone, a few types of salad, egg and meat dishes served in every imaginable way, fish and fruit, and of course copious amounts of alcohol to share.

It quickly became clear that the owner of the house was not the head of the family at this table. His father was, and it was he who poured us the first glass of wine. The toast swiftly followed. Our glasses weren't small; normally this amount of wine would have lasted us a long time, but not in this house. Everyone downed the wine and we were expected to do the same. When in Rome... so we downed it, too. The glass was refilled right away and another toast was raised. The pace was fast and quantities large, so we got drank quickly. Even the language barrier stopped being a problem. With a bit of Russian, Polish, English and German we understood each other well.

It was always the grandfather who initiated a toast. That was a Georgian thing; when it comes to drinking, Georgians have a well developed code of conduct. There's always one person introducing a toast, called Tamada. He (rarely she) ought to be eloquent, intelligent, smart and witty, with a good sense of humour. Each toast is carefully crafted and will inevitably lead to drinking for Georgia, family, being together, women, the dead and many more things. It was obvious that the grandfather was the Tamada in this house. He was chatty, full of jokes and clearly respected by his family. Despite his old age, he was a big drinker and insisted on raising one toast after another in rapid succession. Even the Georgians seemed unable to take that much alcohol without getting smashed.

At one point the grandfather tried to get up from the table. He wobbled and within two steps fell heavily to the floor, hitting his head against a hard metal box on his way down. We all looked in shock as blood gushed from his head. Instantly every member of the family came running, wanting to help somehow. The sons tried lifting him up, but he was barely conscious and standing was not an option. Someone else brought bandages to stop the bleeding. Then, only a few minutes later, the old man stood up and made his way to the bathroom, almost as if nothing had happened. Luckily he wasn't hurt badly, though it looked bad enough to frighten the whole family. On his return, the grandfather wanted to continue drinking, but the mood in the room had changed. The accident was sobering. We didn't want to overstay their hospitality and left shortly after seeing he'd live to see another day.

The following morning we got up late. There was no rush. We had to wait for the alcohol to leave our bloodstreams before getting back on the bike. In the afternoon we knocked on the door to once again thank the family for the kindness we'd received, but there was nobody home. Soon after we packed our stuff and left.

Later that day I had an important meeting in Tbilisi, while back in Batumi two new guests were about to arrive at our apartment.

Though we didn't want to, our best option was to split up. Rebecca got a bus home and I ended up going to the capital.

A bag of luck

"You start with a bag full of luck and an empty bag of experience. The trick is to fill the bag of experience before you empty the bag of luck."

-motorcycle wisdom

I swear there was a magical spell hanging over that bloody sprocket. This wicked piece of metal had turned against us time after time. It refused to leave our poor souls in peace and tried to disturb our lives at every possible opportunity.

Like in every fairytale, this story too, had started far away and a long time ago, when the two of us were still living in Poland. My old motorcycle chain was worn out so, unaware of the dangers that would later follow, I turned to a mechanic for help. I was unlucky, he was a charlatan in disguise. I entrusted my motorcycle to the hands of a total stranger; a decision I would later come to regret. I got my bike back two days later. It was fitted with new sprockets (front and rear) and a chain.

The story should have finished there and then, but the next weekend, when driving in remote villages of southern Poland, my front sprocket came off while negotiating a turn. Hearing a sudden loud noise coming from underneath the bike, I hit the brakes. We were very lucky; I managed to stop the motorcycle just before the chain jammed the wheel. I immediately realised how serious this mechanical failure was. With less luck, we could have even died.

We were stranded in the middle of nowhere, scared about what just had and what could have happened. It was a Saturday evening and chances of a quick recovery were slim. I asked in the village if there was a mechanic nearby. There wasn't. Then somebody directed me to a welder and that's where I pushed the bike, hopeful that it could be fixed in a more civilised way than welding. Oddly, the place was still open and the welder was willing to help. First he tried finding the part I needed to re-attach the sprocket. After searching for almost an hour, he concluded that welding was the only option. He made it clear to me that the process would permanently attach the sprocket to the drive shaft. I didn't know what to do.

Thinking about it, I expected my brand new sprockets, with good care, to last another ten to fifteen thousand miles. That seemed a lot of miles for my old bike. The bike was more likely to die before. Also I worried that the sprocket could fall off again, if it wasn't welded. I had to make a decision, quickly. In the end, it was fear that influenced my choice and logic was merely used to justify it. So that's how I agreed to have the front sprocket welded. There was no subtlety in the welding. It was rough and brutal. The sprocket became one with the shaft, a permanent part of the motorcycle. It wasn't pretty, but it worked. It did exactly what it was meant to; it eliminated the risk. It was done and there was nothing more to think about, except regular lubrication. Was it a happy ending? Not exactly…

All was good for about five thousand miles. Then, one day I noticed that the chain was wearing out far too quickly. I knew that there was some excessive vibration on it, but I believed it was just my bike; it had always shook like crazy which is pretty normal for these kinds of engines. But there was more to this story than I first thought. After some investigating, I realised that the chain vibration was caused by the front sprocket. It was something I'd missed before; the weld was uneven. I needed a new chain right away, and I needed to fix that front sprocket. But I had no clue how to fix it. It looked like permanent damage; the weld was solid.

I asked for advice on the Horizons Unlimited website and was told:

> *That is WELDED... Permanently... You're not grinding that sprocket off without taking the end of the shaft with it. He's turned the shaft molten from the very end. Quite simply.... You need a new shaft.. It's F**ked*

The message couldn't have been clearer; my worst fears were confirmed. The bike needed some serious work and I knew it wouldn't be cheap. I predicted that it could cost even as much as the bike itself. It was bad news, but I wasn't having it. I ignored the forum advice and decided to try my chances at getting the old sprocket removed and somehow attaching a new one.

The story continues in Georgia. It was there that the repair had to take place. I had a set of quality sprockets and a new chain, which I'd brought from Poland (not without almost losing them, twice), so I just needed the right person to fix my welding mistake. A good motorcycle mechanic would have been ideal, but I was willing to settle for a knowledgeable car specialist. A fellow biker from the HUBB came to my rescue. Cliff was from Canada but had lived in Tbilisi for years. He gave me a list of mechanics that he knew were trustworthy. He also offered to help once I arrived in the city. Just after Easter I took him up on his offer.

It was pouring with rain when I arrived in Tbilisi. I called Cliff and he showed up a few minutes later. I was drenched to the bone but just wanted to get things done. Cliff didn't have much time either, so after a brief chat, we went to find the mechanic. I followed his car on my bike and twenty minutes later we were in front of some backstreet garage. It wasn't the place that mattered, though, but the person working there. Kato, the mechanic, spoke only Georgian and Russian, but Cliff was fluent in Russian and patiently explained exactly what I needed. It sounded simple; remove the old sprocket and attach the new one. I feared that in practice it wouldn't be that easy. Kato gave me an appointment for the next morning. It was too late to do the work right away. Just before leaving, Cliff reassured me about Kato's abilities as a mechanic and welder. He also told me to call him if I needed any help. I was grateful to have met this kind Canadian guy.

Soon, I found a cheap hostel and settled in for the night. But I didn't sleep well at all. Throughout the night people were coming in and out of my dorm, but more than that, I was worried about meeting the mechanic on my own. I didn't speak Russian so just needed to trust Kato. It was going to be hard, I knew. And I was scared that things could go really wrong with the bike. In the worst case scenario, a bad welding job could damage the motorcycle beyond repair, which would basically mean the end of our journey as we'd planned it. How could I sleep in these circumstances?

I got to the garage more than an hour before the opening time and waited anxiously. Kato came on time. He was friendly and at the beginning tried chatting with me, only to realise that there was a serious language barrier between us. Shortly after opening he pulled out his tools and began working on my bike. He reached for his grinder first. I froze; that was the moment I'd been waiting for and dreading for a long time. But Kato seemed to know what he was doing. Sparks flew from the grinder as he made his way around the weld. The sprocket was holding up. Minutes later it was as firmly attached as when he'd started. I was losing hope, but Kato was only warming up. Next, he brought a bearing puller from his garage and wrapped it neatly around the sprocket. Grinding, pushing, pulling. Grinding, pushing, pulling. That's all Kato did for about ten minutes. I couldn't even bear to look. At this pace, the drive shaft was quickly turning into dust. And I desperately needed that shaft; at least some of it. Then at last the weld gave in. The sprocket fell to the floor, emitting a tuneful ring. It was the sound of victory. I immediately moved closer to examine the shaft. My body relaxed, before I was even able to process the information. The shaft was still in pretty good shape, with only a tip grinded. The first step, the one I'd feared most, was completed.

After all that grinding, it was time for Kato to have a cigarette break; a well deserved one too. By the time he'd finished smoking, the drive shaft had cooled down. We tried the new sprocket and it fitted perfectly, just needed to be secured. Kato suggested welding it gently onto the shaft. By then I had my absolute confidence in this guy. He said it was the best solution; I listened. He began welding. I watched as he worked with the utmost care and attention. If it were major surgery, grinding could be compared to an amputation, while welding to a complex body transplant. I was impressed and glad that Kato took his time. Before permanently attaching it, he made sure that the new sprocket was properly balanced on the shaft, and he did indeed do a brilliant job. The new weld was nowhere near as deep as the old one, making it easy to remove in the future. I was really pleased.

The job was done. Only the matter of payment remained open. Before he even started the work, I'd wanted Kato to tell me how much it would cost, but he continuously ignored my question. He just kept telling me not to worry, which naturally made me worry even more. I was wary of my situation. I'd seen people being scammed this way, just because they didn't confirm the price beforehand. In the end, though, I stopped asking. There was something about Kato and the situation that made me trust that it wasn't a scam. I was about to find out. Once again, I asked how much I owed and finally got my answer. My jaw dropped to the floor. I didn't know what to say to that; Kato wanted no money at all. I insisted for a while, but he just became dismissive of me, almost offended by not accepting his generosity. I had no choice, my thanks were all he would take from me. I was grateful to Kato, but I also knew that I owed Cliff a big thank you.

Death behind the corner

The motorcycle was fixed by early afternoon. Ahead of me was a long drive back to Batumi. Rebecca suggested that I should break the journey into two days, but I was keen to be home as soon as possible. There were two bikers who'd recently arrived in our apartment and I wanted to meet them.

Getting out of the capital probably took me more than an hour. By the time I hit the outskirts, it started to rain. It was bad news. I stopped at a petrol station to put my waterproofs on and to allow some time for the rain to wash off the road surface. In Georgia, the majority of cars are old and in a rather bad condition, which means that oil spills are very common. Mixed with water, it's a recipe for disaster. It didn't take long before I saw the first accident; some car thrown into a ditch. Miraculously nobody was hurt. But it was just the beginning, a small display of what was coming. I was about to witness some serious lack of imagination, insanity really.

Rain or not, it made absolutely no difference to other drivers; they were speeding just the same. One thing worth mentioning is that having bald tyres is perfectly acceptable and quite common in this country, and I mean wires-sticking-out bald. Driving these cars in the rain is like playing Russian roulette. I didn't have to wait long to find another car thrown off the road, and another, and another. It was carnage. But I continued. I had to. Though at times it felt like walking through a minefield, with my eyes closed. Anything could have happened, at any time, and there wasn't much I could do. Slowing down and being the odd one out was definitely not an option I wanted to explore. So I clenched my jaw and followed the flow, mad as it was. After a while I almost got used to driving like that, until the traffic came to a sudden halt. I had a feeling that it was another accident. The road was narrow, but I managed to squeeze through the traffic jam. Then I saw something I was not prepared to see. Indeed, it was a car accident, a very nasty one. It was an ambulance. It had collided with another vehicle and halfway through its broken windshield there was the desecrated body of the driver hanging out. Chills went down my spine. I turned my eyes away, wishing I hadn't seen this gruesome image. But it was too late; it had already buried itself deep inside my mind.

I wasn't even half way to Batumi, but was already worn out. My previous fears were very much justified; these roads were a death trap.

I wasn't the only one affected by the accident; for the first time that day most drivers kept to a reasonable speed. But this transformation didn't last long. Out of sight, out of mind! Soon enough the Russian roulette began all over again. At the first opportunity I chose a different road; a less travelled alternative through villages and small towns. It would take much longer to get home but it was quieter and safer. I needed to escape the madness of the main road.

By the time I arrived home I was simply exhausted, physically and emotionally. I couldn't shake off the image of that poor ambulance driver from my mind. All I wanted was to embrace my wife and find solace in her arms, but there was no space or time for that. We had guests.

Leaving home

Before leaving Batumi, we agreed to host two final guests. We needed some good karma, as soon we were likely to become somebody's guests ourselves. Besides, we couldn't say no to these guys; they were the first bikers who'd asked to stay with us, and they were both from Poland. From the moment we met I knew we'd get on well, we had so much in common. Simon and Erik, as they were called, were on their way to Australia, only quickly passing through Georgia. It was just the beginning of their long adventure. Thanks to their company, I quickly forgot about the accident. It was probably exactly what I needed; a positive distraction.

The initial plan was for Erik and Simon to stay with us for only a couple of nights, but the plan changed when Erik realised that he'd left his driving license back in Poland. His wife couriered it to our address immediately, but we knew it would take longer than two days to arrive. In fact we expected that it would be about a week, or even longer.

Both Eric and Simon were good company and time was passing quickly; almost too quickly. Soon, we'd all be starting a new chapter of our journeys. Eric and Simon were going to Iran, Rebecca and I back to Turkey and then on to Kurdistan, Northern Iraq. Coincidentally, Eric's driving license arrived just two days before our rent ran out. It was meant to be this way; for the four of us to leave together. The last two days in Batumi were spent drinking Georgian wine, planning our route through Turkey and preparing the motorcycles. Our resting days were soon to be over. None of us could wait.

It was raining heavily the day before our departure, but luckily the sky had cleared overnight and we woke to a pretty beautiful day. It was definitely our time to leave. We reached the Turkish border within an hour. Just before the crossing, we refilled our tanks with petrol. The saving wasn't huge but enough for a couple of meals.

To enter Turkey, we had to pay for visas and bike insurance again. It was getting hot, so being sent from one queue to another wasn't fun. At least this time we were able to keep our passports with us. We were through in no time.

Ironically, our first destination in Turkey was the old Armenian capital, Ani. It took us a long time to get there, but it was worth these few extra hours. The place was huge and the ruins stretched in every direction. We walked for over an hour and had covered only a small part of it. Then, accidentally we discovered an adjacent cave city with thousands of small houses carved into the rock face. We'd never seen anything like this, especially on such a large scale. It felt like we'd stepped back in time. We'd have liked to have stayed in Ani for longer, but there was still a lot of distance to cover that day. Besides, it was scorching hot and we were boiling in our motorcycle clothes.

Not long after leaving Ani, we realised that Eric was missing. We waited for a while, allowing him time to catch up, but he never came. We knew that it couldn't be a good sign, so we turned around and went looking for him. Soon we found him by the side of the road. He'd got a flat tyre. I'd always dreaded being in this situation myself. Theoretically replacing a tube is a relatively easy thing to do, but in practice it can be a real pain in the backside, especially if you don't know what you're doing. And none of us did.

Between our three motorcycles we managed to come up with a pretty decent set of tools. It was a good start. Soon we began fixing the tyre, confident in our abilities. All was going well, till it came to breaking the bead. We wrestled with the wheel for a while, but it was just a waste of our time and energy. In the end it came to the point when we had to admit to ourselves that we needed a tyre mechanic. Simon volunteered to take Eric and his wheel to the nearest city.

As they were getting ready, a car pulled over. Our gear and tools were all over the place, so it probably looked like a motorcycle accident. A man came out to check if we needed help. After explaining the problem, he offered to take Eric to the nearest garage, despite having his wife and kid in the car. It took almost two hours before they returned but the tyre was sorted. After all that effort, the man and his family were still smiling. They seemed genuinely happy to have helped. We tried to thank them best we could, but it felt insufficient. We parted without being able to repay the kindness. By the time we got back on the road, we were almost two hundred miles behind schedule; a significant delay. We had to catch up, but not on empty stomachs. We hadn't had any food for hours and even though it was slowly getting dark, we had to eat before moving on. In the nearby town, where Eric had earlier got his tyre fixed, we found a small place with excellent Turkish pizza. It was what we needed; fast and filling food that was also tasty and cheap.

Once we'd filled our bellies, we returned to our bikes. We were ready to leave when a young couple, probably in their twenties, came over. They were curious about our adventures and quickly invited us to their house.

Eric and Simon hadn't been on the road for long and didn't want to miss out on the opportunity to hang out with some locals, while Rebecca and I felt that we should make a final push for the day. It was an awkward situation. In the end Eric and Simon agreed to leave with us, but we could sense their disappointment. To make matters worse, dark clouds appeared on the horizon. We tried to outrun the storm, but it soon caught up with us. It started raining heavily. Not having much choice, we pulled over by some dodgy stopover for lorry drivers and pitched our tents just behind the building. None of us were happy about the place, but it seemed safer than driving through the storm. We'll never know what we missed back in town, but it was sure we didn't gain much by leaving.

When we woke up the next day, the weather had cleared up. We had a small breakfast and hit the road. For most of the day we kept a good pace. By late afternoon we were satisfied with the distance covered and stopped for a break. We ordered some food in a small local café. As we were eating, the weather changed. Out of nowhere it started bucketing down. It was a relief that we were sheltered. Half an hour later the rain eased a bit. It was our opportunity to leave and find a place to camp. As we were getting ready, the owner of the café told us about a nearby spot that could be ideal for us. He even offered to take us there. We happily agreed and followed his car out of town.

As we were driving, the storm returned. This time it brought thunder and lightning with it. We continued, hoping that we were almost there. But we weren't. Soon the storm came closer towards us. It was right above our heads, striking with frightening regularity, not further than a kilometre from us. We knew that, unlike cars, motorcycles offer no protection against lighting. The situation was seriously dangerous, but there was no place to hide. Scary as it was, we continued. Luckily, we soon reached our destination. Back then, this short journey seemed like an eternity. As we pulled over, it stopped raining.

The spot was great. It was located amongst green foothills that in the distance grew into snow covered peaks. There were hardly any houses around, except one large restaurant. Right opposite, stood a construction site; just bare walls and a roof. It instantly drew our attention as a potential shelter for the night. Having that roof over our heads was almost as good as the prospect of being upgraded to a honeymoon suit. Before making ourselves at home, we went to the restaurant to ask for permission to pitch the tent. Not only did we get that, but also some firewood, access to a toilet and to a water source. Soon our tents were up and the fire was going. It felt homely enough.

Farewell

We woke up to a perfect morning. The sky was cloudless and bright. Birds were singing and the sun was rising from behind the rugged mountains. I made a fresh coffee and milky porridge to kick-start the day. We all ate and drank in silence watching the morning mist slowly fading away in the valley below us.

The air was still cold when we left the campsite, but the sun was gradually beginning to warm it up. Only after leaving were we able to take in the full beauty of the region. We began climbing uphill, steadily gaining altitude. Eventually we reached a point from which we could see far into the distance, the whole area surrounding the mountain. It was a spectacular view. Rebecca and I had to stop, even if for a minute, even with Eric and Simon way ahead of us. A few minutes later Eric joined us. It was a spectacular view; a view that shouldn't be rushed. A glimpse would not be enough. Unfortunately for Simon, he was long gone. We could have stayed there longer, but had to conform to group pressure. That, we did not like. We like to travel our own way; to stop whenever we want, rest often, take plenty of pictures, veer off the path and sometimes even get lost. Eric and Simon were great company, but we were beginning to miss our freedom to travel in our own unorganised slow way. We caught up with Simon half an hour later and from there, all together, we drove to our next destination, Ishak Pasha Palace.

The palace was another picture perfect tourist attraction. It was located high on a mountain, overlooking the surrounding area.

Unprepared as we were, we hadn't checked opening times before arriving and we found the palace closed. Rebecca and I promised ourselves to return there on our way back from Kurdistan, Northern Iraq.

We were getting closer to the Iranian border where the boys were headed. It was finally time to break away and wish Simon and Eric farewell. Someone took a final picture of us all and we parted. To be honest, it was refreshing to once again be on our own. It felt like we'd lost good company but gained freedom; freedom in the form of choice.

Our next stop was Van, a city located some two hundred miles further south. We stopped something like every half an hour, not because we needed to, but because we could.

The next couple of days we stayed in a hotel, where we took time to prepare ourselves for our visit in northern Iraq, mainly Kurdistan. Our knowledge of the country was pretty limited. On the one hand we had a picture of kindness, generosity and outstanding natural beauty painted by our CouchSurfing friends, and on the other hand a dire image of war and tyranny, chemical weapons, oppressed minorities and a nation in turmoil; something you wouldn't find in a travel brochure. One seemed to contradict the other. Was the Kurdish part really so different from the rest of the country? It was hard to believe. We just had to see for ourselves.

The good news was that entry to Northern Iraq was visa free for a fortnight. To extend that period, even by one day, visitors had to go to a hospital for a blood test! Two weeks is not much time to get to know a city, let alone a country, but a blood test was not something we fancied having done. Fourteen days would have to do.

We arrived near the border one day before our planned crossing, ready to enter Iraq as early as possible the next morning. It was a dirty dusty little town, with just a couple of hotels, both as bad as each other. In one of them, we were offered a large discount, so that's where we checked in. We fell asleep unusually early. The alarm woke us up at the crack of dawn. Unlike other mornings, we got up straight away, excited and slightly anxious about crossing over into Iraq. After breakfast, we packed our stuff and went down to check out. The receptionist who'd dealt with us the previous day wasn't there anymore and out of the blue the amount we needed to pay had almost doubled. We'd had a bad feeling about this place from the start. Luckily for us, Rebecca acted on her intuition and when we were checking in, she asked the receptionist to write the price down on a piece of paper with the receptionist's signature just below the amount, so we'd have it in black and white. But it didn't matter; greed fired up by self-righteous anger does not listen to reason. Soon another person came and backed the receptionist. Now the two of them were attacking us.

The situation would have been much worse for us if Rebecca hadn't got the price written down. It was a big day for us and we certainly didn't want to be dragged into a petty argument. We weren't in the mood for that. Against their angry demands, we paid what was written on the piece of paper and left. Ahead of us was Iraq.

- The end -

If you enjoyed reading this book, you can find our second book on Amazon.

Amazon UK: https://www.amazon.co.uk/dp/1973475197/
Amazon USA: https://www.amazon.com/dp/1973475197/

We'd very much appreciate if you could give us a **review on Amazon.**
Thanks you

*Also, you can visit us at **www.facebook.com/nomadsatheart/***

You can also subscribe to our mailing list to hear about our latest books.

http://www.nomadsatheart.co.uk/mailing-list/

About us... where it all started

We met in London, in 2005. Rebecca had just finished her university degree and had been living in London for a good few years. I, on the other hand, was relatively new to the UK, having recently dropped out of university back in Poland. I'd figured that Politics wasn't for me, and as many other young people do, I went to London in search of change. And here the story starts, Rebecca and I found ourselves working in the same pub in north London and we hit it off instantly.

There were many things that drew us together, music and our shared love of Pink Floyd was the first, but it was probably the zest for adventure we both shared which sealed the deal. Within the first few months of our relationship, we'd quit our jobs and jumped on a flight to India for three months of backpacking around the country. It was quite an adventure and turned out to be a real test on how much we wanted to be together, the "make or break" trip for us as a couple. Despite some difficulties; cultural shocks and a few very stressful situations, which included some hair-raising bus journeys, we made it through, still together.

We got back to the UK with what you might have heard other travellers call 'the travel bug', but before we could set off on any other major adventures, we needed to organise ourselves. We blue-tacked a big map of the world on a wall of our studio apartment and marked all the places we wanted to visit. We both found jobs and started saving for our next big trip. I quickly grew fed up with low paid jobs and signed up for a degree in Information Systems and Management at LSE (the London School of Economics). This time, having paid for it with my own hard-earned cash, I stuck it out until graduating. In my spare time, which I had very little of, I studied for other IT certificates. Soon the hard work paid off and I got my first IT job working for the London City Council.

Rebecca was also working her butt off. Her love for other cultures and for learning, led her to do a year-long certificate in teaching English as a foreign language. After qualifying she worked hard to develop her skills as an English teacher, and in her spare time she gave private lessons to make more cash to add to our travel fund.

It was a challenging three years, but by the end of it we'd saved enough to leave everything behind again; this time we bought two one-way tickets to South America. The plan was to stay there exploring until our money ran out.

After an amazing four months spent travelling from country to country, we settled down for a bit in Poland. I got a job as an IT Project Manager and Rebecca continued teaching English. Little did we know that just a few years later, in 2013, we'd sell pretty much everything we owned to embark on a motorcycle adventure of a lifetime.

Having gained some travelling experience over the years, we knew that we wanted more freedom to move around countries. As much as we'd enjoyed "most" of our public transport adventures when abroad, we wanted to break free from this style of travelling and to have more independence. Hitting the road by motorcycle seemed like the ideal solution. It was our ultimate means to freedom. From that point on we've embraced the simple life of permanent but slow travellers. Back in 2013 we became homeless by choice and haven't regretted it for a moment. We feel privileged to live the lifestyle we want and to have the freedom we have. What we value most in life is freedom and we feel blessed not only to have such freedom, but also to share it with each other.

27525870R00068

Printed in Great Britain
by Amazon